# DELLS AND HOLLOWS

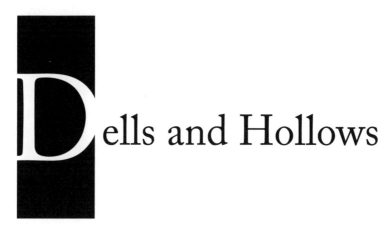

# Dells and Hollows

Poems by Marjan Strojan | Introduction by Sydney Lea

91st Meridian Books

*AB*

Autumn Hill Books
Bloomington, Indiana and Iowa City, Iowa

*Dells and Hollows*, by Marjan Strojan, published by Autumn Hill Books, Inc.
1138 E. Benson Court
Bloomington, Indiana 47401
USA
*www.autumnhillbooks.org*

English translations of "An Important Visit," "On the Stability of Bridges," "The Pope's Letter to the Bees," "The Status Report," "A Sudden Death Delayed," "Remembering Hopkins," and "Where Are You" © 2016 Alasdair McKinnon. English translation of "The Riddle of History" © 2016 Andrew Zawacki.
Poems and all other English translations © 2016 Marjan Strojan. All rights reserved.
Printed in the United States of America

91st Meridian Books is an imprint of Autumn Hill Books published in collaboration with the University of Iowa's International Writing Program

To contact the IWP:
International Writing Program
100 Shambaugh House
430 N. Clinton Street
The University of Iowa
Iowa City, IA 52244-2020
USA
*iwp.uiowa.edu*

Design by Justin Angeles
Cover photo by Jerry Griffis

Autumn Hill Books ISBN-13: 978-0-9827466-5-3
Library of Congress Control Number: 2015947015

*AB*

For David, Gašper and Kristina

# CONTENTS

## IV Dells and Hollows

# INTRODUCTION

**Sydney Lea**

I owe a long and deeply treasured friendship with Marjan Strojan to Robert Frost, my monumental predecessor as Vermont's Poet Laureate. Let me explain.

In 2001, at the invitation of the American ambassador, I gave a reading at the Slovene PEN club in Ljubljana. Prior to my presentation, I was a guest on Marjan's radio show, and immediately found the man's geniality and intelligence magnetic. To my delight, then, he invited me to join him for further conversation at a local café that afternoon. In the course of our talk, I learned that I was speaking with Slovenia's preeminent translator of Anglophone poetry into its language. He had done *Beowulf*, and was finishing *Paradise Lost*, with Chaucer's *Canterbury Tales*—since completed and published—on the horizon.

Marjan had told me he had also been working on the poetry of Frost. As a translator, he may not aim always to be form-true, but he is dedicated to being, as it were, sound-true. In that respect his approach to Frost, known for fierce allegiance to the largely iambic rhythms of colloquial English, had required heroic effort, the cadences of spoken Slovenian being distinctly non-iambic. He informed me, though, that after twenty-five years he had completed fifty poems, and that they would soon be available in book form.

We two stayed in touch, and I was soon chagrined to learn that, owing to an oversight on the part of his publisher in Ljubljana, Frost's American house, Henry Holt, would be demanding an exorbitant and unaffordable permissions fee if the volume were to see a print run greater than 250.

By purest coincidence, my former student Peter Gilbert, now director of the Vermont Humanities Council and also a cherished friend, serves as Frost's literary executor, and arranged for radical reduction of Holt's fee. My part in all this required no more than a terse email, but Peter's intercession on behalf of Marjan's volume redeemed a quarter century's worth of work on his part. Marjan has showed his gratitude, itself exorbitant, by repeatedly contriving to have me back to Slovenia for various literary conferences and, in 2006, by seeing a selection of my poetry, translated by his hand, into print there.

At the risk of over-anecdotalizing, let me leap ahead almost a decade and a half. Marjan and I were walking the streets of Ljubljana not long ago when we came to a church called Trnovo ("a thorny place"). On a stone tablet outside its doors we beheld a sonnet by Slovenia's greatest poet, France Prešeren. It recounts Prešeren's first sight of Julija Primitz, the woman whom he longed—vainly in the end—to make his wife. Julija instead married into a rich German family. Despite Prešeren's being a prosperous lawyer, he was a Slovene, which made him a second-rate suitor in his beloved's eyes. It's a very sad story, but what came out of it was a sequence of sonnets, Marjan tells me, that not even Keats could have composed for Fanny Brawne.

As we stood there, Marjan offered a spontaneous translation of the poem on the wall, and then, having spoken its final phrase, he lapsed into silence, with visible tears in his eyes. My response was a bit self-censorious. *Here*, I thought to myself, *is a man to whom poetry matters in a way that you can't begin to grasp.*

These two developments may indicate the vast range of thought and emotion to be found throughout the book that follows. In our radio interview and in countless discussions since, ones dealing with individual poems and poets, with translation theory, with politics, on and on—in such conversations I have been deeply aware of this poet's learning and his intellectual capacity; but that moment in front of Prešeren's stone tablet implies the ballasting greatness of heart and the depth of feeling that attend Marjan's every thought, gesture, and work of literary art.

A reader coming only, say, upon the ingenious and complex "The Riddle of History" might well wonder if he or she were up to contemplating work of such cerebral scope in more than one poem at a time. "The Riddle of History" is itself riddled with history and erudition, including not only references to but also meditations on the fall of Rome, Greek philosophy, calculus, and Antony and Cleopatra, to cite but a few.

Yet even in this ambitious poem, there exists an undercurrent at once undeniable and elusive. It has something of the magical about it, though that term is imprecise; however it might be described, though, it functions everywhere in Marjan Strojan's canon. In "To a Fish That Took off with My Line," to choose one random instance, the speaker feels his line tauten, then recognizes that the fish has drawn him into a realm beyond his rational ken:

his every pool and pitfall
hates my seeing them: for this is his domain,
his world of strict divisions, split by boundaries,
like farms hooked onto opposing slopes
parts of the same hill and woodland,
each at each other's end, both one. He's pulling
at my slope, my meadow, at my lime tree,
the barns filled up with hay,
pulling the ground from underneath the church ...

While a normal angler might feel a lust for conquest, along with a physical and mental challenge, on connecting with so powerful a quarry, this one suddenly finds his seemingly well-ordered and conventional world being swept from him by a force he is powerless rightly to explain. No, *magic* will not do as a just descriptor, but that great otherness in the world, that complex of inscrutable energies, which is surely beyond definition, resides everywhere, and here is a poet who is forevermore available to it, and to whom it is available.

There need not even be some unusual incident like the hooking of a mighty river fish for the movement from quotidian to ethereal to take place in a Strojan poem. A work I especially treasure is "Imperceptibly, in a Small Room." Early in its presentation, we read that

... man is not conscious
of his moment. He walks the streets, and
the river banks, his friends come to pay him
a visit, they drink tea; the banks and churches
go on with their business, cats keep themselves
warm in the sun; the army is in a state of alert.
Tea tastes like tea, friends discuss football,
the radio is on, parents complain what all this
is leading up to.

Nothing out of the ordinary, it appears. But in Marjan Strojan's poetry, we must always be prepared for sudden transformation:

Imperceptibly, in our small
room things take on a different shape. We see
there is more color to the world than we were
used to taking notice of. Turning the high
street the late night tram utters an indescribable
screech; the language of humans and animals
is transformed into incomprehensible music;
a muted conversation in a café is full of light.

Strojan's sensibility is so keen that what remains imperceptible for the common lot of humanity can for him burst without warning into perceptibility. I'd propose, in fact, that here is a mind for which what we lazily call mere metaphor is vividly, sometimes almost violently alive. An English-language dictionary definition of metaphor might go something like this: "a figure of speech in which a word or phrase refers to a thing or a quality or an action to which it is not logically applicable." But for Marjan, metaphors—indeed all figures of speech—may be as literal as fact. In "On Returning a Book to a Public Library," the passage of the speaker from the routine into the figurative and strange seems gentle and gradual:

...I can't for the life of me
remember who wrote it; even his middle name,
a common and well-known one, evades me
completely. A tiny collection of verse, like
scenes of renaissance architecture and its triangles

and elegant stairways in precise, condensed
light, the color of salt. It was a book of
poems which now, when forgotten, seem even
better, compact in the language of vague,
unruly translation, opening new and unexpected
prospects on each of its metaphors—sharp and
twofold—like "pillars" and "horse."

In "The Status Report," on the other hand, the transition is abrupt:

We stood in front of a building
no different from the one on
the other side. Yet, entering it,
we found our bodies gone;
viewed from back home they
would have looked like strings
of Italian spaghetti, stretching
over the Milky Way.

In the altogether gorgeous "Before the Adagio," for yet another instance, we find this moving passage:

I push open the door and almost invisible I go into
the concert hall. A nod from my professor
of Philosophy, no longer with us.
A little farther forward
sits my professor
of Literature,
no longer
with us.
Now when I see them I myself am no longer there.
I disappear in a moment, but fading out
slowly into darkness like
the scenes in old
films. No more
concert
halls,
no musicians. The evenings have died away,
the nights, too. What constitutes
our existence, what sort of
continuity, when things
end so finally — once,
twice, three
times?

I suppose that to possess a spirit such as Strojan's may be something of an ordeal. Fixities and definites—the sorts of constructs that we rely on as bourgeois—are forever collapsing before him. Continuity, to use his own term here, must be a chimera, and although I can testify at first hand to the poet's suavity, aplomb, and sense of humor as a social being, there is a way in which, given his sensitivity and perspicacity he seems almost an alien among so-called "normal" human beings. This is perhaps one nuance of the final lines, for example, of the beautiful "Zinnias in Bloom"; the poem's nostalgia is lyrical in the purest sense of the term, of course, but its finale opens also onto that other dimension I have been trying (rather in vain) to describe:

> Zinnias in bloom; a train
> moving on, departing: maids'
> work on the balcony.
> An electric pole—a hedgehog
> trying to climb it: a palm tree
> by night. The branch of an elder-
> bush dressing itself up in black:
> the scent of its inflorescence
> quietly glowing. Among the wild
> rose petals a spider hiding from
> the rain. Had it not gone into
> hiding it would have stayed hidden.
> Night gathers; the starlings flock
> onto a sign-board: in the sky
> a child from the long gone past
> is happily singing. Rain descends from
> the heavens; fire licks the star
> by the edges. One me coming down
> to lie on the earth.

Though I have perforce spoken in terms too general to cover all the qualities in *Dells and Hollows*, whose poems can be wry, poignant, heartbreaking, joyous, cerebral—I could go on *ad infinitum*, because, as I said at the outset, the man's range is stunning: though I have largely spoken in generalities, no one reading my words can doubt my profound admiration for Marjan Strojan's verse and his person. Innocent of the Slovene language, I must imagine that these poems are even more compelling in their original tongue; I know, however, after years of crucial friendship with their author, that few men or women are similarly sophisticated when it comes to matters of language. Given how splendidly *Dells and Hollows* reads in English, I must believe these renderings, in all but a few cases the author's own, are more than merely felicitous.

The reader, I am confident, will share in my joy at their availability in the English language.

# ACKNOWLEDGEMENTS

I would like to thank the following periodicals in which these poems, sometimes in their earlier versions, originally appeared:

*The Southern Review*: "On Sun and Sand," "In Wind and Rain"
*The Iowa Review*: "Sudden Death Delayed," "Imperceptibly, in a Small Room"
*The Ascent*: "Imaginary Landscape," "Spring in the Mercator Projection"
*Verse*: "The Riddle of History"
*Words Without Borders*: "Walking"

The poems "An Improbable Incident," "Zinnias in Bloom," "In Equilibrium," "In Unfriendly Weather" and "The Day You Loved Me" first appeared in the collection *In Unfriendly Weather, Four Slovenian Poets* (Ljubljana, Lud Literatura, 2011).

I am grateful to Russell Scott Valentino and Nataša Ďurovičová of Autumn Hill Books and the International Writing Program for their excellent editorial work, and to the Slovenian Book Agency for their support of this project.

However, I owe the present volume entirely to the determination of Sydney Lea, Poet Laureate of Vermont, without whose encouragement and perseverance it would never have seen the light of day.

—MS

# EDITORS' NOTE

The selection of the poems in the volume is the poet's own. Yet in light of the near-uncanny perfection of Strojan's English self-translations, the volume's editors thought it would be worth accompanying at least a few of them with their Slovenian originals: first off, simply to stress that all the poems in the book are translations; secondly, to allow those who can read both languages, even just to some degree, the pleasure of comparison, especially when the theme of a poem is deeply rooted in a specific Slovenian milieu and vocabulary; thirdly, because even readers with no Slovenian whatsoever will be able to see in the shape of some of the poems that the purely formal constraints the poet imposes on himself in one language are resolved differently by him in another. The comparisons will highlight, we believe, the tour-de force that is Strojan's work as a poet and a translator.

# I   IN THE LOW DAYLIGHT

# V večerni luči

Po latah našega križevega vrta so umirale potonike.
Sonce je umiralo za njimi in polnilo sadovnjak
in cesto do kleti z vonjem pregretih marelic
in osutega cvetja. Nič več me ni moglo
ustaviti. Nobena misel me ni pribila
na mesto; nič, kar sem videl me
ni pripravilo, da bi se obrnil
in še enkrat pogledal—
moja glava je bila polna zajcev. Hitel sem mimo
stare mame, ki je napravljala rože za v križ
pred večerom; mimo pasjih kamilic in
kopriv ob ograji, grmov rožmarina,
mimo drobnih, belih kukavic in
prašnih gumbkov in lobelij
in lis strupenega žafrana.
Stric je prihajal naproti
s praznim vozom, z voloma, ki sta majala z glavama,
se trkala in vlekla vsak k sebi; teta je, zgrbljena,
v predpasniku, v krilu in gumijastih škornjih,
s koso čez ramo in z grabljami za palico,
štorkljala v isto smer kakor vsi drugi,
vključno s kokošjo, ne da bi me
opazila. V svetu vonja sem
bil neviden. Preden sem
vedel, sem bil mimo češenj v Dobravi, ves čas na sledi
cvetov svete rešnje krvi, ki jih je Jezus potil na poti
do kalvarije na hišnem vrtu—imeniten na križu
s trnovo krono iz marjetic in s kleščami za
koleni, če bi rad kdaj ponoči in v mrazu
zlezel dol s križa, ko bi nihče ne
gledal. Bil je moje rasti,
a jaz sem rasel hitreje.

## Walking

All along our wooden cross garden the peonies were dying...
The sun was dying on them, too, filling the orchard and
the village road with the scent of warm apricots and
squashed petal leaves way down to the cellar.
I didn't stop walking, no thought would pin
me down, nothing I saw would make
me turn around and look again,
my head was full of rabbits.
I passed by my grandmother, arranging the flowers of the Cross
before evening, I skipped the tufts of wild chamomile
and nettles by the railings, shrubs of rosemary
and islands of tiny white coo-coo flowers,
lobelias and blue buttons and patches
of crocuses, poisonous to touch.
My uncle came along on
an empty cart behind
a pair of oxen, swinging their heads, bumping into each other,
then pulling apart again, with my aunt trailing behind, bent
in her long skirts and rubber boots with a scythe over
her shoulder and a rake for a walking stick—
all going in the opposite direction,
including a hen. In the world
of scents I was invisible.
I came to the four
cherry trees at the Oak Dale's end, following a trail of the red holy-
bloods little boy Jesus was shedding on his way to Calvary
in our front garden, looking  smart on his old wooden
cross with a crown of daisies and thorns and a pair
of tongs stuck behind his knees in case
he might like to climb down for
the cold of the night when
nobody was watching.

Hodil sem in krenil v gozd, ki je brnel od žužkov in muh
v usahli luči dneva. Še malo in bi po Mrzlem potoku
priskakljal v laz, kjer smo nabirali šmarnice
dolgo v poletje. Naprej po robidovi poti,
črni od plodov, je zeval opuščen
rudnik s Krvavim potokom,
ki je vodil na Drugi svet in
za žično ograjo in lopo
je poleti sopla konjederčeva luknja. Izzivali smo se,
kdo si upa tja čez, tak smrad se je širil z med vej,
kadar so imeli odprto. Potem so na piš vetra
v vrhovih bukev in smrek potihnili žužki
in ptice in je kot zmeraj umolknil
potok pred avemarijo z zvonika.
Odzvonilo je; brž je padla
noč. Nič me ni moglo
ustaviti, vendar nisem več tiščal naprej v zid nočne
tišine. S štora na robu jase sem izzival mesec,
naj vzide. Nobenega meseca ni bilo in tudi
zajcev ni bilo od nikoder. Samo tisti
iz glave so se mi pasli okrog nog,
z očmi, ki so sijale v temo,
rdeče od cvetov svete
rešnje krvi.

He was about my size, too, but I was growing faster. I pressed on
following the buzzing of insects and flies in the dying light
of the day, jumping the slant stones across the Cold
Water Creek, where you could pick lilies of
the valley weeks into summer. Farther on,
along the raspberries' path, blackened
by spots of decaying fruit, there
was a chicken wire fence
with a horse-pit and a flayer's cabin behind, hidden from sight.
We dared each other to climb the fence to get the whiff
of the place when they kept it open for business.
Then, on a sweep of chill, birds fell silent,
the buzz and the creek observing
the evensong bell from across
the roof-tops of beech-
trees and firs.
Nothing was going to stop me now, yet my feet would take me
no farther into the night's wall of silence. I sat on a stump,
daring the moon to come up. No moon came and no
rabbits turned up either. Except the ones in my
head, still browsing about my sore feet,
their eyes in the night red with
the glow of the holy-
blood flowers. ◟

## Not in Noah's Flood

They say we write to remember and we read
to forget. Ignorant of either, I wished I could
write to grow up, especially the letter Y.
I've been practicing Y since I first saw it printed

on the covers of American picture books
arriving in U.N.R.A. parcels, safely tucked away
up in the attic. Y never failed to impress me,
looking both like girls' legs pressed together

and the forked sprigs we broke off from the alder
trees to place our fishing rods onto when we were
going after the dace; and in my dizzier moments,
like the throats, slit open by broken bottlenecks,

of long coated dark men in cheery hats, who,
a few pages on, turned into corpses, floating in
booze or drowning in some other disastrous liquid,
but not, for all I could see, in Noah's flood.

## Cats and Dogs

Warm, with my face pressed to the pane of a small
winter window, I, a five-year old, look out at my first
funeral: a thin winding line of mourners meandering
down over the foggy hill behind a white coffin.
He was smaller and much younger than I and deader
 than Lebinger's dog. But I also remember other
days which I could not have seen for myself, and yet
they were there nonetheless. Like the ringing of bells
on a July afternoon in the field of oats overgrown

with cornflower and poppy somewhere out
in the country, the earth splashing, the plough of
clouds hissing, a man trying desperately to unlace
his other boot. Of course, he was still alive when caught.
Now, said one of the captors, we shall perform
a little operation on you. — For you, not to lie too sick
for too long, said the other, pouring down brandy from
the bottle with a wasp caught in its neck on his bullet-
sprayed stomach, like an offering onto one's grave.

I knew him from the photographs, taken in front of
a church or in a garden. The one I remember most
was the one shot in front of a hay-barn, with a guitar.
The guitar was held by his friend, very high up and
at an awkward angle, like a rake held on a steep
slope. Two village yokels, the pair of them, and
both as yet unmarried — though fair to say, my uncle
(with a hello and holding a boot in his lap) was
thrown out of the choir after an alto had stepped down

and left town for an abortion. The second tenor, forty
years old, now and forever. This one is still kicking,

said the third of the party, but the audience did not know
whether this was said of the uncle or of the wasp that
meanwhile had come to life. And I also remember one
of the other days, when we were taken in a school bus
on an excursion to a small ecclesiastical museum,
where in some parallel Universe a depraved bunch
of clerics was torturing members of the resistance.

The photographs of this acquired later a degree of
notoriety. In a series of snapshots one saw a man,
euphoric in shock, in a pair of cross country
knickerbockers, with white eyes, with black lips,
with his hands tied behind his back, being killed
with a loggers' axe like a pig in the snow. I came
down with a fever every time he appeared (for
the death of me — a spitting image of the crackpot
with the guitar), hanging from a butcher's hook all

dressed up as St. John of the Wood. It is only human
to be hung up like this in times like ours, said my uncle.
Quite, said the Church with the Museum. And justly so,
for all humans in photographs become more human
after the passage of years. We assure you these are
all fakes, says the child in a coffin, smaller and younger
than I. But why then, asks the peasant with the guitar,
am I still sick? Because the wasps have stung you,
says St. John of the Wood, dead as the Schrödinger cat.

# To a Fish That Took off with My Line

The bite of morning chill like a blind flash,
the first thrust of his weight connects the brain
with water. A power, flat and deep, unknown
that grips the line and straightens the long arch.
A tightening that cuts into the bone
of something shooting up the neck, poised
for the feeling of the shiver at the other end —
feeling his tail, the drag of his fins, his running
sideways, a stubborn snout, its surge upwards
against the river-water, hard as rock,
sand-grey, as old as the Alps. A crazy moment —
not of happiness — more one of triumph
and the fear of loss creeping down my legs,
nothing but instinct telling me my end
of the rod from the other end, wrestling with my
pebbled stand, with the sun surging upwards
into the lower ranks of poplar, resisting day
becoming night that rolls the boulders
along the bottom of his realm.

Where each spring and each brook that ever flowed
into this fish, his every pool and pitfall
hates my seeing them: for this is his domain,
his world of strict divisions, split by boundaries,
like farms hooked onto opposing slopes
parts of the same hill and woodland,
each at each other's end, both one. He's pulling
at my slope, my meadow, at my lime tree,
the barns filled up with hay,
pulling the ground from underneath the church
I'm holding in my hands against him stuck

in shallows water willow trees that have gathered
by the will of their old roots into my fish.

Who turns, and turning snaps at hard won years
of boyish wait that are no more a play
of comings and goings, learning the quiet
horrors of disappointment. Of expectations
in the first moment of a grown up man,
in the last moment of the river. All these
I have caught back and will pull out to hammer
with stone and throw onto my shore.
To open up this moment, crush the head,
be free and light again—hooked onto nothing,
just me alone, myself; to leave the river bend,
roll up my line, straighten the arch and my
own reckoning with myself. And watch as he,
gliding an inch beneath the surface, brown
as a trawler, leaves the harbor and sails away
on his dangerous, unfathomable routes,
where there is nothing but fish and fish.

## Thirty

He sat on a trunk of a young spruce cut down
one Sunday afternoon — the woods still blue
and trails dug up by wheel-tracks all around
too wet for anyone to pass through.
He liked the tight feel of his shirt, the dell
all quiet and the solemn cool of things
at ease that this first Sunday's sunny spell
had brought to the belated Spring.
But it wasn't all woods: from the spruce over the hill
flung into the air resounding with May
a cuckoo's call plunged through branches at will
like a doe through fern-grass — not calling to stay.
He reached for a cigarette, tapping for matches
to light up and to listen. He did listen until
all at once there was nothing; the song came in patches,
windblown on the wing of the air that went still.
He looked up the slope; from where snow kept its ground
it stared back at him, too deep for too long
for him to light up, sure that next time around
he'd keep score of the calls of a faraway song.

## Poklic

Če se na kaj razumem, je to umetnost
čakanja. Čakanja nisem nikoli opustil,
čeprav je v letih mojega ukvarjanja
z njim dočakalo temeljite spremembe.
Prva stvar, ki se je spominjam, je bilo
neko otročje, enkratno čakanje brez
večjih posledic. Nekaj drugega so bila
čakanja na mrazu, da bi smel v hišo,
ki so bila prav tako časovno omejena,
a so se po nekem nočnem pripetljaju
spremenila v izkušnjo s posledicami:
v spanju si še zdaj pokrivam ušesa

z vsem, kar mi pride pod roko in spim,
dobro spim, samo na desnem boku
in na desnem ušesu. Čakanje sem vadil
v gozdu, ob reki in bajerjih, v kevdru,
na cesti in v gmajni, kjer se je dobro
obneslo, in seveda sem komaj čakal,
da zrastem, kar mi je šlo malo slabše,
a to samo za uvod. Svojo umetnost
sem jemal resno, iz veže sem zlezel
na podstreho in tam po lestvi na tram
in po njem v sleme in k lini, od koder
sem videl do konca vasi in po cesti

do mlina na eni in klanca na drugi
strani, z vmesnimi strnišči in travniki,
z reko, potokom, brvjo in jelševjem
ob potoku, s hribi in nebom nad reko.
Gledal sem vse to v dežju in v snegu
in v večernem soncu poletja; imel sem

# A Calling

If I ever excelled at anything, it was waiting.
I never gave up waiting, though in my many
years of polishing the skill it changed thoroughly
from its unassuming beginnings. The first
incidence of it that I recall seems like a childish
prank of no lasting effect, but there were more
to come. Like waiting outside in the cold to be
let in, which, however restricted in scope, was an
experience with all the effect it entailed. In bed
I still cover up my ears with anything I can take
hold of, and can sleep, sleep well, only on my
right side, on my right ear. I rehearsed waiting

in woods, by ponds, by the river, in the cellar,
on the open road and on the common where it
paid handsomely. And I couldn't wait to grow up, which
didn't go all that well, but as they said, it was
a beginning. I played the game earnestly from
the outset. I climbed the narrow stairs to the attic
and from there by a ladder onto a beam under
the roof-top and down to a dormer-window from
where I could see the water mill and stubbly
fields with patches of grazing land at the far end
of the village and — over the river — the manor
house and the brook, the alder trees, the hills,

and the sky above them. I watched these in rain
and snow and in the evening sun of summer.
My eye was good, though. I could see rows of
black beans and sweet peas in the garden plots
next to the market church, carpets of crimson
alfalfa carried away by bees to the distant

tako dobre oči, da sem razločil grašico
in fižol po vrtovih, preproge lucerne,
ki so jo čebele raznašale po travnikih,
ali — v oblaku prahu — strica na črnem
kolesu in psa, ki je dolgo dirjal za njim
in nazadnje obstal. Gledal sem ženske,

ki so s cekarji hitele od maše in, redko,
od mesarja, in ko je čez reko izginil
vlak za ovinkom, može, ki so se z ruzaki
in klobuki vračali iz mesta. Videl sem
lovce in ribiče, ki so se po dva in dva
s puškami in palicami luščili iz megle,
si pokimali in se razkropili v grmovju
in po gozdovih. Videl sem župnika in
ministrante, ki so s kadilnico in križem
bežali pred ploho in gasilski avto, ki je
zakuhal v klancu in se je zbrala vsa vas.

Za razliko od gasilcev tovornjaki niso
bili redkost, a so največji vozili ponoči
in nam odnesli kos strehe in pol ganka,
ki ga potem nihče ni pozidal. Z mamo
je bilo podobno, nisem je videl prihajati,
kar stala je v veži, rumena kot sončnica
in ko sem zaspal, izginila kakor kafra.
Za mesec, dva, tri, do velike noči ali
do velikega šmarna, kakor je naneslo.
Štel sem dneve, si na prste zapomnil
njihova imena v tednu in v letu, videl,
da se vse ponavlja, ne da bi se ponovilo.

Vmes smo kuhali šnops in otrobe, orali,
sejali, sadili krompir in spravljali les,

meadows, my uncle pushing a black bicycle
under a cloud and a dog chasing after him for
a while and suddenly stopping. I watched women
with their straw bags going from mass and, rarely,
from the butcher's; and, across the river, with
a train gone behind a turn, men with backpacks

and hats coming from town. I saw hunting and
fishing parties with shotguns and fishing rods
turning up in pairs in the fog, nodding to each
other before getting lost again among thickets
and woods. I saw a parish priest and his altar
boys with their censer and cross running away
from the storm. And a fire truck blowing up on
the rise with the village crowd gathered to watch.
Unlike fire engines, trucks were a common sight,
though the big ones passed through only after
nightfall, taking with them a slice of our roof
and a chunk of our entrance steps which no one

ever bothered to put back—just like my mother,
whom, too, I never heard coming until she stood
there in the doorway, yellow as a sunflower,
gone again into the night as soon as I went
to sleep—gone for a month, two, three until
Easter or the Assumption Day, whichever came
first. I counted days on my fingers, remembering
their names in a week and their place in a year,
getting used to things turning up without ever
returning. In the meantime we made schnapps
and boiled bran, put potatoes to earth, cleared
woods, drove timber, lit commons with fires,

plowed, sprinkled manure, mowed, made hay,

kurili v gmajni, polivali gnojnico, kosili,
sušili, želi, mlatili, ličkali, trli koruzo,
prešali, klali, točno kot ura. Disciplina
čakanja je zahtevala mnogo posebnih
znanj, ki jih je bilo mogoče vsa piliti
v nedogled: nositi vodo in drva, pasti,
napajati, obračati seno, grabiti v kopice,
okopavati, pleti, nastiljati, kidati gnoj,
nakladati, furati, izpreči, žeti za zajce,
zvoniti opoldne in zvečer, ni bilo konca.
Težko se je bilo znajti v tem krogu,

se pregristi do imen za stvari ali si priti
na jasno o čemerkoli. Posrečilo se je
samo včasih, kot recimo, ko sem njeno
nenadno pojavo in skrivnostna izginotja
povezal s sanjami in se odločil, da čim
se prikaže, ne bom šel več spat. V celoti
načrt ni uspel, v podrobnostih pa sem
vendar izsilil, da bom, kadar spet pride,
smel z njo. To je bila nova disciplina —
čakanje z obljubo, ki je zdaj prevladala
in v kateri sem brez lažne skromnosti
dosegel določeno stopnjo popolnosti.

Kmalu sem se prvič peljal z vlakom in
tramvajem in smel shraniti vozne listke.
Videl sem prvomajski sprevod, zaprtega
strica v pižami, redi kostanjev v cvetu.
Ni minil mesec, pa sem že silil nazaj.
Tako sem še večkrat čakal, da končno
odidem, in ko sem odšel, da se vrnem;
čakal na pisma in dočakal, da so nehala
prihajati; čakal nekoga, da pride, dokler

reaped, threshed, husked corn, pressed cider
and vine, slaughtered pigs, regular as a clock.
Waiting entailed many skills: to carry in water
and logs, graze and water the beasts, rake leaves,
strew, shovel, drive a cart, un-harness, unyoke,
turn hay, build stacks, hoe and weed furrows,
cut grass for rabbits, toll bells at midday and
eventide — no end to one's waiting. It was hard
to keep ahead of tasks while running in circles,
to sink teeth deep into the names of things,
or clear one's muddle about anything, really.

It did happen once in a while, though, as when
I tied the riddle of her comings and goings to
dreams, determined the next time she came
I would not be falling asleep. On the whole,
the plan was a failure; in detail, however,
I squeezed out a promise that she was to take
me with her when she came back. This kind
of waiting, waiting on a pledge, was to become
my new shiny discipline, my chief one from
now on, one in which I can immodestly say
I excelled to a degree of perfection. Soon I rode
train and tram for the first time, allowed to keep

my tickets to the end of the ride. And I saw my
First of May Workers' Parade and my uncle
in his pajamas behind the Houses of Court,
an alley of chestnuts in bloom ... However,
not a month passed and I was already pressing
for home. So I was waiting to go ever after
and, when I left, waiting again to come back;
waiting for letters to arrive until they stopped
coming, or waiting for someone to call on me

ni za zmeraj odšel, ter nazadnje dočakal,
da je nekoč proti jutru zazvonil telefon.
Takoj sem vedel, kdo kliče in se zdrznil,

ker sam že tako dolgo nisem poklical.
V treh korakih sem se spomnil treh
razlogov, kako in zakaj ne, v četrtem
sem začutil takšno olajšanje, da sem
pozabil vse tri. Čutil sem, kaj sem ves
čas pogrešal—kako se moj prefinjen
občutek za čakanje ni dal…ni obstal
pred nemogočim: čakal je dalje v temi,
pepel, brez znakov življenja. Preden
sem stegnil roko, sem že slišal njen glas,
kako me ošteva. Dvignil sem slušalko—
in jo položil nazaj. Telefon ni zvonil,

a klic je bil pravi. Poklicala je, kakor je
edino lahko, drugi ne kličejo več niti
v sanjah. Dočakal sem, da sem nehal
čakati, kakor sem nehal čakati, da bi
se vrnil gor v lino. Dobil sem škrlatinko,
ko smo v šoli ravno jemali pisanje in,
čez čas, zlatenico. Nekaj časa sem bil
v karanteni, potem so vprašali, če hočem
domov. Pol leta sem preživel v hiši na
koncu vasi, kjer sem imel lepši razgled
kakor z line pod streho. Prerasle so jo
veje. V njej ni bilo nič, razen marelic.

until there was no one to call; when one night
towards morning I heard the phone ring. I knew
who was calling, I winced for not giving a ring

there myself for so long. In my three steps to
the phone I invented three excuses why I hadn't;
with my fourth I felt so relieved that all three
were forgotten. I knew what I'd missed all
these years, how my sense of the game never
gave up on me, not giving an inch against
the unspeakable odds, waiting on in the dark—
ashes, no sign of life. Even as I reached for
the phone I heard her voice scolding me for
the failure. I picked up the receiver and put it
back down. The phone hadn't rung, but the call
was real. She called the only way she knew,

others don't call anymore, not even in dreams.
I waited it out to put an end to my waiting, just
as once I have ended the ache to return to my
place up on the beam. I caught scarlet fever
and then—as my class were learning to write  —
jaundice, and had to be put into quarantine
before being told to go home. Then, after I left,
I came to live at my aunt's house at the end of
the village, where for the next half term I had
a better view of the world than from the dormer
window under the roof. Now it was overhung by
a tree; apart from apricots, there was nothing.  ◥

## The Magi

There wasn't much I knew about the church—half an inch
of it on an old Valvasor copperplate showing his manor,
and even then it was called St. Catherine's. Before her it was
Sts. Cosmas and Damian's, but those two were now left
sulking at the side facing the snake herding St. Margaret
With a Chain, having full view of St. John the Steadfast being
thrown from the bridge. I wondered what the chain was all
about and was told it helped with the weather at haymaking,
and that judging from the rivulets of blood oozing from
a disused mine nearby, St. Barbara or St. Nicholas must have
once stood in her place—Nicholas being the patron saint of
log rafters. And while we're here, the painting still reminds us
of the dangers of high waters, St. Nicholas's church now stands
half an hour from ours and there's plenty of Barbara and her
wheel in a mining dell behind the Baron's other estate where
they bred co-op horses. I recognized the key to the church

door at once. We used to put it in a pitcher with wormwood
and water to heal gnat and mosquito bites. I was made to run
back to fetch it whenever I was stung by a wasp. "Get ready,"
he said and gave me a push over the doorstep. I gasped. Inside,
the church smelled like a saw-mill. From the side altar to the seats
in the nave a mossy hill soared up that you could sled on; along
its ridge ran a towering wall with scarlet coated legionaries
armed with short swords, with Diana's Temple and the palm
trees half covering the Confessor's bleak hour under the bridge …
"I'll switch on the lights." It was drizzling outside, but in here
it was bright. "Don't have to," I said; even without, one could see
everything—a water mill leaning against the slope, the first
of its kind I was aware of, with a flume and a pond, water lilies
and carp and shepherds making camp fires on the hillside.

Hellebores, which the sheep cleverly skipped, were pushing
uphill and coming down the slope a bearded herdsman in

a brimmed hat carried a bundle of deadwood ready to burn.
Above, a handsomely built angel held a white and gold band
inscribed *Gloria in excelsis Deo*. Back on the road stood
a friendly inn where under the shade of horse chestnut trees
a Bedouin company sat at a game of cards. Five Meissen
singers were coming from the graveled road with notes
and instruments. Over these, and all else, hung the Italian sky
from which twinkled more stars and angels with trumpets
and captions in gold, but this was merely the beginning…
The church lit up, a small choir softly intoned "Look up,
the stars of heaven" and white Toulouse geese and Pekinese
ducks circled the pond. The scent of frankincense flowed in
from the sacristy; on a hillside in a mossy grotto appeared
a gleaming scene with a donkey, a pair of oxen and Mary
and Joseph on their knees and a baby Jesus raising his arms
to the comet as if touching his fate. A trickle of a stream ran

onto the wheel and with the sound of piss in a urinal wiggled
off into the pond. At a stroke of a hammer a nearby smithy
lit up; black miners with picks and axes were pressing into
the shafts or were hanging around on the side. From the ducks'
pond to the mill under the fortress a line of support columns
and wires sprang up like soldiers, and a loggers' cable-way
carrying bundles of firewood started uphill. There it dawned
on me where in this compromised country of hellebores and
date palms the shepherds' fuel supply came from—a fact of
economy no doubt contested by angels and legionaries, with
all sides engaged in a treacherous struggle and no end in sight
if it were not for the recurrence of a solemn event—a Christmas
tree descending on the manger without anyone knowing how

it came about. "Wait! It'll get stuck," he said, giving a kick to
a stack of brushwood under the rails. There started a frightening
clamor and on an oboe solo from behind a turn, on horseback

and camelback, a party of Magi appeared on the rail-track with
their train of servants and dogs. The first among them, a Venetian
Moor of noble demeanor and genteel appearance in a starry coat,
a turban and a crown was pointing to the star above the mine shaft
before disappearing into the tunnel. "Engine belt's slipping,"
he apologized ... Then the lights went out, the music stopped,
the scene froze. "The rotor of a scrap washing machine, the rest
I got from across the border." On our way back he explained
it seemed cold enough for the sight to last until March when
he meant to set up a new one based on the same principle if it were
not that he had to give way for Candlemas and was running
out of time as it was. "And what do you do with your life?"
I didn't know what to say. Compared to this—"Nothing," I said.
"Come again," he went on as if he wasn't surprised. "It's worth
having a second look. Two weeks, I might still come up with
something. If I'm not in, the key's under the step stone as always."

**Pogrebci**

Nazadnje zvem, da imajo v vasi prostor —
poklical me je, bratranec, čokat,
siv, majhen, šestdeset, mogoče več,
in sam — tako kot vsi. In zdaj edini
od osmih, ki je še ostal: vsi drugi
lepo pospravljeni okoli jezer
od Kanade do Združenih držav.
Poklical je. Kar je lepo od njega.
Vedel sem, da bo, in mu to povedal.
Zarežal se je, jaz pa ne. Takoj
je vzel nazaj. Deset let je razlike,
dovolj, je mislil, da mi da nasvet —
ta "prostor," sobo, še do lani skedenj,
a zdaj pozidan, bel in zastekljen
in zrak zasičen z vonjem svežih barv,
težak od lakov in zaščitnih smol.
"Vsi pridejo. Je čisto zraven cerkve."
Res je bilo. In res so vsi prišli.
Piščanec ni bil prida, trd, zažgan,
brez skorje, v sredi še surov in juha
mrzla kot kamen, preden smo posedli —
vsi, razen župnika, ki je popil
glaž slivovke na vrtu, se opravičil
in šel…z desnico v mavcu do ramen.
Bolelo ga je pri povzdigovanju.
Vino pa ni bilo zanič. Izpil
sem ga požirek, ko sem videl, da so
vse oči uprte vame. Kakih sto.
Šlo mi je na živce. On je tu glavni,
strokovnjak za stvar…jaz, jaz samo sin,
glavni med žalujočimi, če to obstaja.
Vstal sem, izpil in šel iskat stranišče

## The Funeral Party

I didn't know the village had "a place"
until he called. A cousin, sixty plus,
grey hair, plump, short, a loner like the rest.
The only male I knew (and there were five
in my aunt's family) who stayed behind.
The rest of the boys all neatly spread around
the Lakes in Canada and in the States...
He called. It was a decent thing to do,
I somehow knew he would, and told him so.
He chuckled, but I didn't. He went tense.
Still, with ten years' difference between us,
he thought he'd offer me advice. A place.
A room—a barn I guess, now bricked and glazed,
the air still heavy with a smell of whitewash
and newly coated woodwork. "They all come.
It's right beside the church." It was. They did.
The chicken was bad, the crust burned on the wings,
the other side undone, red meat half-cooked,
the soup stone cold before we were all seated—
my kin and village—all except the priest,
who took his slivovitz out on the lawn,
emptied his glass, apologized and left.
He had his right hand plastered to his shoulder,
had trouble saying mass and was in pain.
The wine was good, though. I just had a sip,
when putting down the glass I saw all eyes
fixed on me, and one hundred of them, too.
I hated this. Damn, *he* was the chief mourner,
I...I was just a son, the chief bereaved,
if there were such a thing. I stood up, drank
and went to find a toilet, shaking hands
on my way through the bar. In there a boy

in stiskal roke celo pot do šanka.
Za vrati, pri umivalnikih je fant
montiral vtičnice za vse prihodnje
rodove neobritih gostov, željnih
skupinskih brivskih srečanj pred straniščem.
V tišini sva si hitro umila roke
in se v zrcalu srečala z očmi.
Nasmehnil sem se, prvikrat ta teden.
Zdaj spet prihaja: tokrat s kelo, z vedrom
in še z nasmeškom za stranišče znance.
Vrag vzemi župnika! Ne bom govoril.
Na tej pogrebščini res ne. Vsaj on
bi lahko vedel, kaj je prav, če ne
že vsi. A kaj res ne? V desetih letih
sem bil na najmanj toliko pogrebih —
več, na enajstih — v cerkev, k jami, k šanku …
in, če pomislim, le na dveh porokah.
Naša stara zgodba: nikogar več
ne vleče pred oltar, samo še v grob.
Smo spričo tolikšnih izkušenj vsi
eksperti za pogrebe … in za žalost?
Najbrž res ne in tudi ni pomembno,
starejši tukaj so bili na vseh:
"A kap jo je? Zdaj smo pa mi na vrsti …"
V obupu sem z očmi ošinil fanta.
Pokimal je in jaz sem vstal, da jim
povem v obraz, kar mislim, da jim gre.
Nič v zvezi z mano — z dejstvom, da pustili
so govoriti žalosti o sebi.
Najbolje, če bom kratek, brez ovinkov,
in če takoj začnem. Začel sem z mizo
in razpostavil v red kozarce, krožnik,
pribor, zložen prtič z božičnim vzorcem.
Nazadnje sem razumel, v čem je stvar.

was putting in the sockets on the sink wall
for future shaving parties in the gents'.
We washed our hands in silence and were leaving
as our eyes hit the mirror and we smiled
briefly, I for the first time in a week.
Now, there he was again, and with a chisel,
a bucket and a grin for his old loo-mate.
Oh, damn the priest! I wasn't here to give
a speech on mum, I couldn't ever, could I?
*He* was supposed to know, but weren't they all?
As much as I was. In her last ten years
we've been to—what?—ten funerals at least.
No, surely, more than that—fourteen, I'd say—
church, feast and all. And, it occurred to me,
in all those past years there were but two weddings
that I came to attend. The story of my nation:
nobody marries, everybody dies.
Does so much practice here make one an expert
on all things funerary, or on grief?
It doesn't really, and it doesn't matter,
they all attended all, and knew as much.
I sent the boy a glance of desperation,
he nodded and I rose, intent on speech
they would remember—not the words, not me—
the fact they shouldn't let grief speak on grief.
I'd better make it short; and tidy, free
of all my usual swaying back and forth.
So I began with tidying up the table—
the plates, the forks, my glass, setting them up
in line with Christmas napkins, when, at spoons,
it dawned on me what this was all about.
She was the last—there was nobody left,
not just among this party, in the village,
in this whole country of her generation—

Bila je zadnja. Ni nikogar več,
ne tu, ne v vasi—zadnja iz tistih časov
in tistih krajev. Petnajsti otrok
v hiši pod cerkvijo—to jim povem.
Nikogar, razen redkih znank, vse v letih,
v črnini, in mene, ki sem tu na pol
domač, in z nekaj šolami...Kot on.
Zahvalil sem se jim, da so prišli.
Vem, da jim ni bilo lahko, sem rekel,
pustiti košnjo, zdaj, ko vsak dan lije,
kot včasih ni. Bilo je sedem sester
in sedem bratov, ki so, razen strica,
vsi preživeli vojno, celo dve—
ki jih vzredila je ta hiša, dokler
ni izčrpana obsedela križem rok...
Tu sem se ustavil. Kdo sem, sem si rekel,
da pridigam, *kdo* bil je kdo, in kaj.
Odšel sem, čas je šel, ti so ostali,
delili si življenje, smrt, grobove.
Pogledal sem jih, sédel in pozabil
nazdraviti spominu rajnkih duš,
kjerkoli so. Nihče ni protestiral.
Prijeli so kozarce in izpili.
Zato prišli so sèm, zato so tu.

of fifteen siblings downhill from the church.
Not many here that she had known from youth—
some cousins, women wearing black—and me,
who was to fit their sense of the occasion,
half farm-half school, next fittest to the priest.
So I began with thanking them for coming.
I know, I said, it's hard because of hay,
raining on every good day afternoon
the way it never did. She was the last,
I said, the youngest in the nest to leave
with all but one surviving two great wars—
all home bred, home raised by the house until
worn out it crossed its arms and let them go ...
And there I stopped. For God's sake, who am I
to tell them who *they* were. I flew away,
time flew before I turned; they stayed behind
and shared their lives with many of my name
to whatever end they came ... I sat down failing
to raise a glass to their poor souls wherever
they might have gone. No one protested,
they all said "Cheers" and drank theirs to the bottom.
That's what they came for and that's what they got.

# II SPRING IN THE MERCATOR PROJECTION

## Spring in the Mercator Projection

Winter retreated, and as the mountain
ridges were closing in on the sea cliffs —
there, at the time of the first recorded use
of a subordinate clause in the language,
sprouted the crossroads of pathways
and winds. From its subterranean vaults
ice traveled on galleys to Capri and
Ischia, some of it even as far as Egypt.

In lunar temples wet nurses required
the sacrifice of pheasants; on splendid
shores ad hoc libraries were built of
sandstone, their departments flaunting
the names of the heroes of the Argonaut
expedition. True, the obstinacy of the local
gods perplexed the conquerors, frustrating
the advance of the natural sciences into

their heartland, which kept returning
expeditionary parties in forms of herbaria
and dancing bears long into the night.
And we mark at the approach of the dawn
as the history of the place was beginning
to melt with its surroundings, how
the monastic orders kept producing ever
new forms of matriarchate, and in their
books of maps we continue to read into
their fondness for ornithology and theatre.
Then, as the word for the atlas was finding
its way into vernacular — busy making
pacts with rich cities overseas by calculating
the grid in which all directions crossing

the meridians at the same angle were
changed into parallel lines, none of them

representing the nearest route to anywhere
on the map—we see its founder cutting
their heavens to pieces, corrupting any
conception they have held of their rivals.
By the time the quotation marks enter their
correspondence we find the Emperor's
Nightingale singing among the fountains
of the park and the Great Prince of Muscovy

making Aesculapius an onstage offering
of a rooster. And as the old amber routes
reopened and the new conqueror was given
lease to crown himself in several churches
at once, instead of bread and salt the citizens
were bringing him buntings. But the simple
truth is none of their treaties ever held water
and no peace they concluded outlasted the dawn.

## An Important Visit

*by Admiral Nelson and Lady Hamilton, on their return from*
*Haydn's Mass No 11 in D minor, at Eisenstadt, in 1800.*

I recall a snowy evening, when a wonderful sledge-coach
bearing a coat of arms stopped in front of the only illuminated
building in town—a hostelry displaying on its signboard
a painted monster called the Elephant, though in the general
opinion it represented Leviathan—and when a monkey,
all covered in snow with a turban and a lighted torch,
hopped down from the seat. It opened the red and gilded
door of the carriage through which emerged a silken foot
in singing shoes under the ermine lining of a dark coat.
Many recall how on the other side her Lord, in his plumed
Admiral's hat, with scarlet piping down the side of his tight
trousers and wearing black lacquered boots stepped out

into virgin snow, overtaking her just as one of her small feet
was about to touch the step, and caught her tiny gloved hand
in the air as she waved to us, pressing it to his silver breast
so that in the carriage-door appeared a blue fur hat with a pearl
and a white peacock feather under which one could see a face
with ruby lips, teeth of alabaster and a swan neck. His Lordship,
who by an indiscernible nod of his head and by lightly clicking
his heels saluted the servants and other staff pouring out of
the hotel (some of them in their aprons), was still firmly holding
her hand level with his epaulette as she with the other hand
lifted her coat to brave the snow to the entrance. But already
the grooms were at hand to help with the horses and gear, while

others hurriedly laying down crimson Persian rugs borrowed
from the music salon, were sweeping doorsteps and staircase.
Numerous windows were opening with maids beating dust

out of bed-quilts and with whole clusters of curious guests
hanging out of them, some of them toppling over into the street
below. Since there was snow in abundance nothing much
happened and no one got hurt. What did happen, however,
was something else. A large sperm-whale (*Physeter catodon*),
making a stop at Tyre on its way to the Sargasso Sea, spewed
out onto the pebbled beach myself, my father and the prophet
Jonah, with whom I had been since early autumn splitting
logs in the vaults of the monster to make ready for winter.

Furnished with these, dipped in tar and happily lit up for
the occasion, the hotel personnel were lining the floors for
them, while the rest, headed by his extraordinary flunkey,
escorted them upstairs to the dance hall, where a temporary
reception room was prepared for the pair. Later, I often went
to admire the red snow-coach in the City Museum where,
changed after the earthquake into a kind of hollow moldering
pumpkin as brittle as parchment, it is preserved to this day,
while as for the whale, it could be seen only when it was
exhibited in the University Park one hundred and fifty eight
years after the event. Their arrival was noted in gothic letters
in various imperial newspapers, but in none that I could read.

*Translated by Alasdair MacKinnon*

## Carl Linnaeus Looking at the Swallows

In the low daylight, merging with the line
of the horizon, downwards stretching
flocks of birds sweep in to the rushes and
plunge into the evening depths of the lake.
A little later the north wind lengthens
the shadows and shortens the paths.
But God, just now working with all speed
on the world, with every drop of rain
on the surface broadens into infinity
circles of new questions, more dangerous

the farther they are removed from the center,
where, as He commanded, Adam's tongue
named the beasts. Should Brazilian mermaids
be put with *sirenia* or in a class of their own?
Is the lizard sent by the mine doctor
in Carniola with the help of the Society
of Jesus a larva or a form of an adult animal?
Why does He pose these riddles? And with
the Jesuits' help? Does He want to draw
our attention to something we have overlooked
or to rebuke our vanity? And then, the swallows.
One thing holds good, though. They rise from
the fresh mud of the lake like dragon-flies
when in spring they feel the urge to return home.
A good thing they haven't far to go, otherwise
they would be scattered wandering the world
and even those that avoided winter storms
would never have found their way under the roof
of The Royal Society of Naturalists. Faithfulness
may signal the lack of a free spirit.

*Translated by Alasdair MacKinnon*

## Imaginary Landscape

As is the case with many good inventions,
his, too, was a blend of quick insight and
happy coincidence. When studying works
of other masters — a couple of them were
his countrymen, even neighbors — his eye
was drawn to the backdrops at the rear of

the set in front of which all painted action
took place (extravagant battles, biblical motifs,
grand nudes and portraits), all seemingly free
of time and events. He knew painted cities,
high cliffs and far prospects behind them
were as often as not done by different hands,

but he couldn't care less. Until now he'd met
no living centaur, no roaming apostles,
and had in the past successfully avoided
kings and battles on high seas and on land.
He contrasted his subject with life and after
years of scrutiny came to the conclusion

that backgrounds were something he could
rely on. His art of the time is thick with
indifference to motive, which many presume
to be insincere. However, it was not until
later when, painting by painting, his objects
were moved ever farther away from their

set focal position (getting blurry in their
carefully poised correlations) that his panels
acquired meanings which seemed to defy
his clients' orders. Sunk into darkness

or breaking away from light, his imaginary
vistas and puzzling interiors were changed

into something that, for us, represents a lost
or forgotten memory, but in a way that makes
it impossible to see whether it was ours
or his. A fantastic landscape in front of which
you are standing "repeats a dream you can't
quite remember but are unlikely to forget." ◄

## Imperceptibly, in a Small Room

Swedenborg reports that, in a way of speaking,
the act of passage is a matter of detail.
When he is no more, man is not conscious
of his moment. He walks the streets, and
the river banks, his friends come to pay him
a visit, they drink tea; the banks and churches
go on with their business, cats keep themselves
warm in the sun; the army is in a state of alert.
Tea tastes like tea, friends discuss football,
the radio is on, parents complain what all this
is leading up to. We imagine that the time

of the passage is shrouded in mist, because
our senses die off, etc. Then there is also
the possibility of death making them sharper.
But it is not so. Imperceptibly, in our small
room things take on a different shape. We see
there is more color to the world than we were
used to taking notice of. Turning the high
street the late night tram utters an indescribable
screech; the language of humans and animals
is transformed into incomprehensible music;
a muted conversation in a café is full of light.

Still we carry on as if nothing had happened.
We keep up with our dates, with our musical
recitals, with our Sunday outings to the lake;
every so often we go to the movies
or to a theatre. But we don't pick up phones,
since the contents of the calls are known to us
in advance; we read books in languages we
never learned. We notice the florist

whom we have last seen in our childhood
giving us a nod of recognition. There would be
un-posted letters and complete strangers arriving

at our doorstep, we would speak to them under
the passageways, on the rooftops and terraces,
in the suburbs, where, had it been otherwise,
we would have never cared to venture. All this
can last for weeks, for months, even years.
By then one is made aware of who the callers
were and what he himself has become; he
makes ready for his moving away, takes leave
of his friends and relatives, who seem strangely
unbaffled by his decision. Then comes the day
when he takes off in one of Charon's buses

and riding with a strange taste of copper in his
mouth comes into a high valley of fens and gorges
with big cities and towns, many of them devastated
and charred as if consumed by fires. The sky
is dark and deep with no stars and no sun. Soon,
without realizing how, he starts coming to
an office, finds himself a job, recognizing in his
superiors the visitors of his unlikely conversations.
His is a world of conspiring and hatred, fast
decisions and summary injustice, where everybody
gets promoted and nobody seems excessively

unhappy. A place of blooming opportunities
and uninterrupted promotion. On one occasion
he takes part in a secret meal where they are
shown the world of the sun and celestial
bodies, which he rejects. Then, on another, they
visit the park opposite the music school where

he used to teach and where he now watches
the undergraduates, entangled in the network
of time, sitting on a lawn, resonating like
an old piano concerto he remembers from a long
time ago. He declines any suggestion of return.

## On Returning a Book to a Public Library

I'll make this short. Days always surprise me.
So when I'm returning a book to a library
it doesn't mean I've finished it or had no
intention of reading on. It only means that
despite its renewal the library's lease has
expired and that the times and places and
extravagant fortunes of men, with the traditions
of various schools and institutions of knowledge,
secret societies and writings of all ages,
collected and arranged into chapters

or classified according to their alphabetical
order, have found themselves locked behind
the doors of inscrutable hallways, keys flung
away as carelessly as if they were dandelion
seeds. No doubt they will go on along
the corridors of some cerebral Hades weaving
their lives quite independent of those that
time and again I capture in my glimpses
scattered or overheard in chunks of
fragmented conversation, however inadequate.

So, in the cobwebs of Saint Petersburg's
Railway Station (in snow) Madame Karenina
still waits to throw herself under a train.
And I'll probably never find out what Vronsky
could have done at the time, if anything.
Tatiana never finished her letter, though I presume
she had turned down the poet, who ages ago,
in his small neat hand, had been scribbling
in his notebook the names of his lovers.
And doctor Rieux, even he—what did he,

after the danger had passed, say to a writer
whose fast travelling ladies clattered around
Bois de Boulogne in their carriages — if indeed
he survived the ordeal? Is this important?
I don't know; take the book I was bringing
back this afternoon. I can't for the life of me
remember who wrote it; even his middle name,
a common and well-known one, evades me
completely. A tiny collection of verse, like
scenes of renaissance architecture and its triangles

and elegant stairways in precise, condensed
light, the color of salt. It was a book of
poems which now, when forgotten, seem even
better, compact in the language of vague,
unruly translation, opening new and unexpected
prospects on each of its metaphors — sharp and
twofold — like "pillars" and "horse." There was an air
of something conquering, victorious in far away
places about them, like a clang of a sword drawn
from a scabbard: *Vincente Cortázar Paladio.*

## On the Stability of Bridges

We may safely say the following: the Greek bridges
were—like the Sumerian temples, the water-clocks
of Egypt, etc.—constructed according to a different
subject and principles of thought. Later, it was found
that they agree in some detail with the currently valid
calculations laid down for the soundness of buildings
and bridges. However, it has now been clear for some
time—and most recently from Poincaré's lectures
at the Faculté des sciences—that today, despite
all the exertions of Byzantine cardinals, Masonic

traditions and the expertise of Babylonian, Arabian
and Indian scriptures, there is no way to construct even
the simplest of gangways so that they comply with the pristine
laws of construction. Another set of rules then governed
Nature. According to our present day experience
the shimmering stars and the planets shining all through
the past systems, their rolling of balls, their running
of years and the fleeing of their peoples would have
sunk to the hub of the galaxies if their previously
calculated ratio of forces had prevailed (Lemaître, 1927).

In contrast with music, poetry, chess, etc., the nature of
calculus has been changed beyond recognition. Triumphal
achievements of mechanics have been thrown to the wind
and nothing much can be said of the onetime order of things
except that it was, judging by the physics of the day,
completely beside the point and that many even doubt
its existence. It seems that our learning follows the changes
in the laws of nature with the precision of an algebraic
sequence modified by the conjectured constant of deferral
to the observed facts (Tomamori-Nakayama, 1958).

But even here the calculations are consistently at odds
with many of the all-important details and at the same
time subjected to methodological shifts, time and again
based on self-generating mistakes (Cavendish, Hill et al.,
1981). So, we can conceive of two identical bridges,
remote in time, but standing close by each other and
sharing the same oscillating frequency, as being
pounded into the depths by the entirely different paces of two
marching legions trying to cross over—an incoming one
and one other that has already left (Blue Superior, 1996).

*Translated by Alasdair MacKinnon*

## A Woman's Destiny

The necklaces against rabies she
wove throughout her first life
are kept in the Cairo Museum.
Two with pendants of Isis and
Horus were later sent by mistake
by the Eastern Church as their
contribution to the fourth Lateran
Council. Then, in Napoleonic times,
a Pergamon parchment was found,
a gift from Mark Antony, containing
an identical female figure and a provenance
traceable to Burcheion, where 1800
years earlier she had taken up a post
when her first collection of verse
was hailed as a modest success.

From her position she kept watch
over the careers of her more
prosperous colleagues,
and the followers of Zenodotus
whose learned little poems she transcribed
into various tongues, some of them
utterly incomprehensible. Numerous
unpleasant incidents were thought
to have been subtly connected with her life
and work, such as the disappearance
of a number of Academy members
and staff, their falling ill, losing
pets, parents, life, inspiration and such.

Slowly but steadily her black
heart had seeped into the walls

of the Museion and the King's palaces
nearby, leaving the Theatre and
the Serapeon choking with rot.
It gathered itself into a black cloud
over the Temple of Poseidon, reaching
as far as the swamps of Mareotis,
until it hung like a shadow over
the entire city, and as the decay
took hold within the Library buildings
of Cleomenes, so her influence grew.

At the moment when one of her
poems left all the critics who had
read it poisoned and dangerously
ill, the gods had had enough.
They consented to get rid of her,
but as is the way with the gods, they
could not come to an agreement
as to the means of her dispatch.
Finally, they used their most
devastating weapon, a well-kept
tactical secret, the accuracy of
which had been demonstrated only
in a select number of cases.

When, at a solemn occasion of
presenting accolades she was
standing in high heels in a puddle
in the draughty Hall of Calliope,
she was struck by lightning.
In the spasm of her enlightened last
wit she dictated a poem which,
by decree of the Writers' Guild, was
to be kept safe under lock and key.

Access to it was denied to all except to their annual Secretary General, but so far no one has dared to exercise the dreadful privilege of reading it through. ◄

## The Riddle of History

I'm not the first to discover the riddle of history.
The discovery in fact occurs daily but to no real advantage.
Supposing that because of improvement in tools,
research continues to yield results as quickly as today
or more so, then the riddle of history will be made
known to pretty well everyone by tomorrow. At any
rate it will be possible to recreate conditions in which
it is meaningful to search for the riddle of history.

But that is all. The riddle of history is not hard
to untangle. Yet, ultimately, it defies all expression.
Let me suggest a theoretical and absurd case,
for it follows from the riddle itself that it allows
only for the theoretical and absurd cases. The history
of the Roman state may be represented by a complex
cryptogram containing everything we know about it.
For example, according to Callimachus' successors

the Ptolemaic libraries in Alexandria catalogued
twice as many books as there were people inhabiting
the city. And every year, the taxmen collected at Faros
from oil, vine, wild honey, silphium, tar, slaves, etc.
just how many denarii in gold – six hundred thousand.
We can think of the command and the way
to try and find the connection, or order the search
for other similar connections in other cities and towns

of the immense empire in its thousand years long
history. The result might have yielded valuable
references as to the riddle of history, but there exists
a major probability that for the obscurity of presentation,
large number of imponderables, interference and

marginal conditions in critical numerical operations
no one would know how to interpret it. It could
be blown apart by one single equation, founded on

a product of two big prime numbers: even the biggest
of tools would have taken years to manufacture
such a product. The code therefore seems to be
an insoluble problem. On the other hand, however,
we may through procedures, common to the practices
of decoding the riddle of history, enter a datum that
Rome sank into decay not because of bad weather
disarray in public services, lead in the plumbing,

mismanagement of revenue office, the transfer
to Byzantium, etc., but rather because of a half-wit
calendar priest from whom from the very earliest
she inherited a numerical system with alphabetical
notation. Regardless of the fact that even while building
an arch the Consul had to put his trust into a precarious
formula for cement and the blessing of the keystone,
and despite any number of the calendar reforms

they had, they let fall into neglect the practices
of fasting philosophers arriving at Rome via Egypt
and opening stalls on the field of Mars almost
from the days when Caesar and Pompeius had it walled up
with theatres. Their eastern system (the only thing
of value in town which Crassus was not trying to buy)
depended on the careful subscribing of numbers
and their determined yet changeable meaning within

each position in the whole operation, and not
any more on one's dexterity with tablets and beads.
It was founded on number 10, for 11011

they needed five numbers (but only two digits).
Besides, their business mind told them
there wasn't a thing which subtracted from itself
would have exceeded naught, and with a little
education they would have been quite capable

of calculating more on a single rainy afternoon
than they would have had in Tabularium in one whole
year. Considering that the Greeks who but for a few
Phoenician letters also did not conceive of special signs
for numbers, but were nevertheless glad of theory,
predicted that the biggest prime number did not exist
(and, also, why not), the mere fact that mathematics had,
by August 1989, succeeded in producing as the biggest

known number of the kind $391528 \times 2^{216193} - 1$,
seems to be a disaster for history regardless
of its being a triumph of science. It appears
that history is moving within the frame of the theory
by which some initial discrepancies spread out
into unimaginable results on a higher level
of iteration. In our case the critical point was
irrevocably reached by the time when under

Maxentius the city registered 1870 villas (*domus*),
46605 blocks of flats (*insulae*), 11 aqueducts,
1352 fountains, 865 public baths, 23 equestrian
monuments, 80 gold and 84 bronze statues,
29 libraries, 45 brothels, 10 basilicas, 424 smaller
sanctuaries and temples (*aedicula*), 290 warehouses,
and grain depots (*horrea*), some 254 water-mills,
1 coliseum etc. None of these, however, have any bearing

on one another or on the whole we call Rome;
rather the relation between any of them seems to be
founded on totally arbitrary grounds. Absurd as it is
the fact is it exists, and that we can effectively think
of it and represent it as such. But think
of Mark Antony on his flattened sand elevation
above Actium, looking over the calm of the bay from
Cleopatra's tent ("Your love is as sweet as Cyprus"),

taking a count of Octavian ships closing to block
his exit; and gathering in his head the last loose
remains of his fractal generation calculus to find out
what method to use to establish how many times a butterfly
would have to beat his wings back in Rome to produce
a windstorm over Epirus at dawn. And if the little yellow
ones he used to chase back in Illyria with his uncle
Gaius Antonius would also do, but that was such
                a long time ago.

*Translated by Andrew Zawacki*

## Musical

He, young and beautiful, stepped out into
the world to make it dance to his tune.
Being a musician he used his inspiration
to bludgeon his wit with characters
no one had ever dreamed of using before.
She, being a muse, solidified the object
of her will into an instrument of her daring.
After the years they spent in murdering
each other's voices by the disparateness of their
talents (and the likeness of their means)
his world turned sour. He kept noticing things
for what they were, which, inadvertently,
he called experience, seeing her mortal airs
growing grey hairs all over the place,
bloodshot eyes, bitter lips, flesh-tearing
talons. He watched her musical thirst
invading his lines to feed on his words,
insatiate with the effort. He thought of himself
growing notes like this and dismissed
the idea. When for lack of a better solution,
he left her with nothing but his "body of
faded associations," she, after a few drinks,
crept back into the desert, and after a while—
being young and beautiful—took a deep breath
and went out into the night in search of prey.

## The Pope's Letter to the Bees

Until very recent times there existed in the West a memory,
containing a word — or at least, the last chance of a word
in the West. In the years when the Moors broke through
the Pyrenees, there was on the French side, huddled in
the shadow of the mountains, a little monastery, where
there lived a man unwilling to bow to the new order.
His actions, sooner rather than later, cost him his life.
Nobody knows how he came to lose it or what heroic deeds
he performed in his remote solitude, nor for how long.

All that has come down to us is a tale, according to which
his executioners, who kept him locked up in a nearby village,
cut off his head; yet he did not die, but like St Dionysus before
him, he made his way to the grave he had dug for himself
beforehand in the mountains. The man therefore takes his place
in a series of younger *cephalophores*, the distance of whose
last headless walk after decapitation may in some instances
be computed, and which in the above case was estimated
to be some three miles long, giving Mme du Deffand
an excuse to have said "*Ce n'est que le premier pas qui coûte*" —
a remark that, as you know, has become proverbial.

More interesting, however, is the continuation of the story,
for soon after the incident there gathered over the saint's grave
(made famous for its healing powers and remission of sins)
a swarm of bees, stinging all who ventured close to the site.
They tried all conceivable means to drive them away,
burning brimstone and rocks, boiling tar, lighting fires,
leading processions and generally creating such racket
and stink that the Caliph of Cordoba had to step in, urging
the abbot to act against unruly worshippers and the bees
whom neither bad weather nor sticks would drive off.

The abbot, himself at his wits' end how to act, turned in panic
to his bishop and since even he seemed unsure what course
to take, the event didn't take long to come to the highest of ears.
Rome, herself conscious of the Caliph's advantageous position
in the affairs of the bees (which the Quran for their industrious
character deploys in Paradise to bring food to the blessed
in the embrace of *houris*), considered long how best to
undertake the delicate task. Finally, through autumnal mist
the ambassadors were dispatched to the abbot with a letter
and an order to have it read thrice to the bees over the grave.

The letter contained some very powerful words, and if we
take into account not the moral, which only tries to instill some
respect into wavering authority of the involved but rather
the excellence of the story, the last such powerful words
in the West. When it was read to them for the third time in
the prescribed fashion the bees withdrew and heavy downpours
extinguished the fires in the woods where they took refuge.
After that they disappeared; they simply decided to sever all
ties with men and long after the letter, the grave and even
the saint's name were all forgotten, some previously familiar
flowers and plants were not to be found on those slopes.

According to tradition the sting of a bee was long thought of
there as possessing healing powers, but only on the condition
that the one who was stung was not in love. Of lovers it was
said that they would swarm like bees over the grave, a phrase
proverbial in the hills but now long forgotten. Since soon after
the memory of it had died out, the bees returned, it is likely
that in a manner of speaking it retained the words which
drove them off. So, the letter read to them in utmost secrecy
        may now be remembered only by the bees.

*Translated by Alasdair MacKinnon / (emended by the editors)*

## The Status Report

We stood in front of a building
no different from the one on
the other side. Yet entering it,
we found our bodies gone;
viewed from back home they
would have looked like strings
of Italian spaghetti, stretching
over the Milky Way.

A few more unpleasant things:
we were struck by the same
question at the same time, i.e.
is our present position a physical
fact or just the result of an operation
within a pure thought experiment?

As we entered the building, the time
pointers showed us in different
directions, but we went up in an
elevator. It stopped in front of an
empty room with a dimmed mirror
inscribed "Museum of Causality."
It was obvious there had been
no one there for a long time.

We stepped out onto a terrace,
but it allowed us no view worth
a mention. A surly caretaker
was busy, hastily sweeping
lost memories under a rug,
much to our amazement leaving
ours untouched. He left us with

our sick mothers, with our
uncertain offspring, with our
own unstable childhood.

When he turned his back
on us his back read *Carry on
as if I'm not here.* There
were other signs, though,
like the smell of iodine on
a deserted beach or echoes
of interpolated sentences
as after a storm, as well as
a firm conviction we were
in a big city. Yet it was
anyone's guess where they'd
come from, or if there was more
to them than just a superficial
exchange of ideas. Rain.

We were aware of our
free will but we had our backs
pressed against the wall:
try to explain to an apple falling down
a steep slope — whose free will
is to turn round in the air
and float back to its branch —
the extent of the notion.

What finally left us in no doubt
was the lower floor scene
with the Creator, beleaguered
on all sides and brought before
the tribunal (which, technically
speaking, was an Inquisition),

absently answering for
himself "Eppur si muove."
And ever since, one is obliged
to express oneself on almost
anything in metaphoric terms,
the sensation that we were
a rainbow from the two
time-bent banks of the river.

*Translated by Alasdair MacKinnon*
*(emended by the editors)*

## On Sun and Sand

Very odd this, with the sand and the sun.
One day the crystals will win, the silicon
ones, the glass. But then the sun will win,
red, thick, at seven hundred million degrees
changed into iron. In the end darkness
will win, absolute, at absolute zero—
hollow, no stars. The denouement is fixed,
come day or night it is the same in the desert
and on the seashore, in this or in the other
worlds, and it concerns me no more than

the astrological signs or the revelations of
Hayley's Comet. I kick the fire and
walk past the sleeping guards back through
the town gates. On his last night one is
allowed to camp out under the stars. As yet
nobody has run off far enough not to be found
a couple of hours after daybreak. My fortune
has no direction and no boundaries, and cannot
be escaped. I am limited by an infinitesimal
fragment of time, though not so tightly that I

would not walk the courtyards in search of my
murderers of today or would evade lying down
in a circle with them, equal among equals,
different only in this—that I have seen through
the optics of my limitation. Morning, which
creeps into my bones, works in all directions
of time. Even with the events taking a different
course, for me, somewhere, this very moment
is lying in wait: the sun will rise, I close my eyes,
     the grains of sand counted.

# III   IN WIND AND RAIN

## In Wind and Rain

It's cold and windy and it's drizzling. Soaked
and sullen, we hesitate to open our umbrellas.
As soon as we do they turn inside out and try
to flutter away with a shriek. Last time I was
here a grand piano suspended from above
the main entrance was opening up with a sharp
rattle like a great mechanical butterfly, uttering
clanky music at incomprehensible intervals as
it descended upon our heads. Then followed
a lecture in which it was said that only a thin

layer of reality still separates us from seeing
our instantaneous present artfully reproduced
a fraction of an instant before it happens. Somebody
from the audience argued back that such a thing
had already been tried (he didn't say where),
and that MoMA had long ago obtained for its
collection some of the finer examples of the genre,
with fatal results. Further polemics have led us
to believe that all portrait painting renders
its subjects stranded in that same position, though

one can as well reverse the argument and refer to
a case at the National Gallery, where the visitors
to the room of Rembrandt's self-portraits fell ill
with an intense feeling of being pursued from
one corner of the room to another by twenty-two
pairs of identical eyes before being silently,
unaffectedly, attentively, roguishly, etc. escorted
through the door, and the compensation claims
of the afflicted personnel had, on all levels, gone
on for ages. Come wind, come rain, people would

come to see anything. Finally, the smell hit us.
Here we were in a white, luminous hall squarely
divided into large containers filled up with naphtha,
looking down into a speckless black mirror of
the architecture above, which, slightly curved, also
contained you, but in far deeper, more perfect
outlines than your usual three-dimensional image,
which half an hour earlier had worked its way out
through the crowd and not yet fully awake had made
love to your wife in the small hours of the morning. ◀

# A Sudden Death Delayed

I was trying to do three things at once. To read the time
away, to smoke less, to ride as far as I could. The blue
lights were coming on in the first class carriage. The red
Chinese lantern sank into the poplars. Awkwardly, into my
pleasant compartment a poet was trying to get, whose book
I had just put down. It was lying spread open on a pull-out
table like a dead bird on a deserted beach, its lines shyly
facing the board under the window, meaning the world.
In it were bridges with canals silently rising and falling,
there were tufts of highway grass and waterway traffic signs
shooting up. "*Stai caminando fin' a Trieste?*" barked
a young man in army fatigues, proceeding onwards, or rather
backwards (considering the direction of the journey).
He was looking older than his picture and as if out of touch

with his comings and goings. He must have had a suitcase,
which now, having found himself a place to sit, he was
eager to return to and bring in, when he saw the book.
"*Stai aspettando fin' a Torino?*" barked another young man,
who could not get on past the poet (nor back, considering
the direction of the journey). "*Entra! Entra!*" He inspected
his own face on the cover some thirty years younger, cut out
and blown up from the photograph, showing him in a circle
of the unknown standing in front of Louvain University.
He mumbled an apology, nibbling (characteristically)
the corners of his moustache, slowly closing the sliding door
to shut himself off from me, or rather, to shut me in from him.
I did not recognize him immediately. I felt I had seen him before
and that, having found his seat in my compartment,

he had only gone out to come back with his luggage.
"*Molto gentile,*" said an elderly blonde to her younger companion,

who, shoving herself through the door and obediently choosing
a seat opposite hers, could not take her eyes off the book.
Hers was certainly a very beautiful voice, controlled and
clear. "*Non si tormenti, le prego.*" Passion destroys passion;
we want what puts an end to wanting. The book was lying
there, facing its windowpane negative. Where there had been
crows, the young night was by now setting in, turned upon
itself, flying away on the reflection of the covers, illustrating
the glazed glass with the ornaments of an evening. *Portoguaro*,
it was an international train, calling at all stations… I saw
him again in the morning, leaving the train as if descending
into someone's embrace. By then of course I had no doubt

who he was. I too would not care to share a compartment
with a stranger who knew so much about me, and carried
an image of my younger self round the world with him.
I watched him disappear among the platform crowd into
a neon mist at the exit. I wondered what he was doing now
in Milan. "*Lei è molto gentile,*" repeated a woman behind
me whom I was trying to help from the train with her bags.
Not really looking I stared down the far end of the platform,
then returned to my own world. Skimming through life on
the inside slip of the cover, I noticed he had died five years
before. I remembered a poem of his, portraying his own death,
and how young I was when I first read it. It described the pre-
war oarsmen and the paddle steamers at Vevey. For the first
time, that night, I was only a step away from immortality.

*Translated by Alasdair MacKinnon*
*(emended by the editors)*

## Nedeljsko popoldne

Na trati njegovega ljubkega kolidža v Cambridgeu sem vprašal
znamenitega profesorja, kaj si misli o vsem tem. Pili smo čaj,
ravno je pohvalil mojo angleščino (na osnovi zelo nepopolnih podatkov),
in ga je vprašanje (v napačnem pogojniku) rahlo
vrglo iz tira. A samo za hip, in čeprav je bil znamenit profesor,
si je vzel čas in mi odgovoril z zgodbo o oslu in škorpijonu,
ki sem jo takoj prepoznal, ker jo je Akim Tamiroff nekoč
pravil Orsonu Wellesu. Mogoče ne ravno o oslu in tudi film
sem že pozabil, gotovo pa je bil zraven škorpijon in zagotovo
je šlo za zgodbo o nepomirljivem in nepojasnjenem sovraštvu.
To pojasnjuje vse. Potok in osla in ravnanje škorpijona,
ne pojasnjuje pa odgovora na moje vprašanje.

## Confidential Report

On the lawn of his lovely College in Cambridge I once
asked a well-known authority what he might make of all this.
We drank tea and he just chanced a kindly remark
on my linguistic skills (based on his deficient familiarity
with the facts) when the question, made difficult by my
erroneous use of the conditional, put him slightly off track.
But only so for a second, for then the professor, regardless
of being a celebrity, took time to respond with a story of
a scorpion and a donkey, or was it a toad?, which I found
vaguely familiar. I thought I recalled seeing Akim Tamiroff
telling it to Orson Welles, but it might have been the other
way around and the title, too, slipped my mind. Yet here
he was with his wild tale of the scorpion and its inscrutable,
but foreseeable demise. I suppose that explained everything —
the stream and the donkey and the conduct of the scorpion;
what was left unexplained was why hate was the answer to
a badly posed question.

## Gutta serena

Kje vse me že niso tepli, na žive in mrtve, kamor
jim pade. Hrasti se mi podirajo na glavo, skoznje
poganja jutranji mesec, namočen v roso. Vstanem,
prižgem luč. Goščava na pol poti sredi življenja.
"Vsaj nog mi niso amputirali," rečem. Spomnim se
sebe, kako me v nekem življenjepisu vsakič spet
znova prebunkajo kakor v nebesih, tako na zemlji.
Proti jutru, z roso. To bo! — Nič ne bo, razložijo:
udi, ki jih pogrešaš, bolijo še bolj. Amputiramo samo
zdrave organe. Pripeljejo zrcalno komoro, kamor ti
vtaknejo štrcelj, ki ga življenje (ki verjame, kar vidi)

zmotno zamenja z zdravim organom in mu odleže.
Utvare! Teh smo potrebni, kje so? Bile so jih cele
knjižnice, nekdo jih zanalašč trga iz knjig. Vsem na
očeh me odprejo in mi v njihovo fantazijsko škatlo
zložijo notranjost, kot da ne znajo šteti do dve.
Takoj se mi stanje izboljša ... A kaj, ko me hrasti
tolčejo po zobeh in mi zdravje požiga jutranja rosa!
"Ne meni se zase, v paniki se celo ščinkavci zatečejo
k netopirjem, bistveno je, da držiš glavo pokonci."
Vseeno, nocoj so mi glavo pretepli kot psa. Še zdaj
ne vem, kako zgledam in zakaj se temu tako reče.

Zdi se mi podlo pretepati pse, ampak privoščijo si,
spremenijo me v psa in me spustijo iz škatle s pasjo
glavo na človeških kolenih. Potem prebunkajo še ta,
a jih smem vsaj obdržati. Zob pa ne, vztrajajo, tako
smo se danes zmenili. "Človek brez zob ni več isti,"
rečem na vratih. "Ne pretiravaj, imel boš pasjo glavo
brez zob, mi smo zadovoljni. Skrajni čas je, da narediš
nekaj zase, lahko bi ti z roso pretepli oči." Takoj grem

## Gutta Serena

There's no place on earth they did not beat me. They beat
the hell out of me, coming down on me wherever it hurt.
Timbers of oak crashing onto my head, the morning moon
shooting through, soaked in dew. I rise, I switch on the light:
a forest halfway through life. At least my legs were not
amputated, I say. I remember how in one of my biographies
they beat me up with eyebright and dew towards morning
on earth, as they do in heaven. "So, this is what happens," I say.
"Nothing happens," they explain. "Imaginary limbs hurt even
more, we only amputate good ones." They bring in a mirror-
box into which they put what's left of one's limb, which life

(believing what it sees) mistakes for the good part and is relieved …
Phantoms! That's what we need. Where are they? Someone
is tearing them out from the books! There used to be libraries
of them. They open me up for anyone to see and lay my bare
insides into their fancy box as if they can't count to two.
At once my condition improves. Still, oak branches beat at my teeth
and the morning dew burns away my health! "Don't take notice,"
I say to myself. "In panic even finches fly to the rafters for cover.
Just keep your head up!" Last night, though, they pounded my head,
they beat me like a dog, and I still don't know what I look like
nor why we say that. It seems foul to beat up dogs, but they

take their pleasure, they make me into a dog and release me
from the box with dog's head attached to my knees. Then they
hammer those too, but at least I can keep them. "Not the teeth,
though," they insist, "that's what we've agreed on." "Man with
no teeth is altogether a different animal," I say at the doors.
"Let's not go into that, you keep your dog's head on the leash,
we are satisfied. It's high time you do something for yourself,
we could pound your eyes with more dew. …" I go to see Doctor

k zdravniku. Tipam v temi, dokler ne pridem. Na stolu
že ima pacienta. "Gutta serena," me veselo pozdravi,
ko šamponira pacientovo glavo. Vprašam naslednjega,

kaj to pomeni. "Okvara vidnega živca," hitro prevede
in zavrti stol. Zagledam profil Johna Miltona iz druge
izdaje, in iglo, ki jo brivec v mraku žari na špiritnem
ognju, preden mu jo tik ob očesu ne zarine do živca.
"Da mi ne trznete," reče in ponovi postopek, ki prvič
ni dal rezultata. " — Kako je to mogoče?" se čudim,
a si brž pokrijem usta, ko se spomnim, da pacient sliši.
"Ko bi videl, kaj delajo s tabo, bi trznil," zašepetam.
"Tako je to s poezijo," odmahne zdravnik, brivec in oče
in otrese prt z umitimi kodri v zrak ali v eter, kdo ve ...
"Pridi, prihaja zora, da ti z rožnimi prsti prešteje rebra."

at once. I grapple in the dark until I'm there. In his chair there is
already a patient. "*Gutta serena,*" he greets me shampooing his
patient's head. "What does this mean?" I ask the one next to me.

"A defect of the visual nerve," he promptly translates, turning
the chair around. I see a profile of John Milton from the Second
Edition, and a spirit burner and a needle glowing through
the darkness visible before he thrusts it into his eye socket.
"Don't budge," he tells him, repeating the procedure which
at first attempt produced no result. "How is this possible?" I protest,
covering my mouth as it dawns on me the patient can hear me.
"If you saw, you'd budge," I whisper. " — It's all poetry, lad,"
says the barber, the surgeon and father in one, flapping the towel
with ringlets of hair against the air—or was it ether, who knows?
"Go, here comes the dawn to count your ribs with rosy fingers." ◄

## The Dark Star

We live behind the Hospital for Contagious Diseases,
back in the fifties. Ours is a ground floor house,
low down and yellow. To enter you go to the back door
past the woodsheds coated with mortar and turned
into homes. Next to them stand a latrine, a sink with
a brass tap, and a leaky motorbike in an unlikely state
of repair. The backyard is laid with gravel and slag
with a hopscotch left drawn in the sand from the summer.
Along the railings gray linen and chequered bed-
covers flutter from the rope to dry. You can hear
everything. No one is out. The sun is setting. We fight.

You rush through the door, leaving the curtains and
glass on the door-window shuddering. You splash
water onto your face. No one comes to your side as if
the police may arrive any minute. It is likely I am
the police. There's an officer's hat on a table and a chair
pulled down on the floor with a brown chicken perched
underneath and a *džezva* coffee pot turned sideways.
You wipe your neck with a side of your slip. I lie low.
I can't see where I am and I'm not behind the barracks
door either. I'm hidden so deep I can't make myself out.
It seems there's another room farther back; maybe

I play at not being there; maybe I reckon they'll think
you beat yourself up; they know you like to provoke.
Then out into the yard walks a child resting its hand on
its officer's belt. In its other hand it carries a bicycle
light. I know at once it is me. It threatens you with the belt.
You scream. You start back to lock yourself up. Next,
you throw the police hat out into the yard. A chicken
comes to peck at it. You look good, slender, with a long

neck and washed up eyes. I see an eclipsed red star rolling
down from the invisible universe come to the ground.
I kick it towards the playfield, then fall for the game. ◂

## By the End of the Day

The rule is simple. A game is fair if the stakes match the wins
and you stand a chance of winning at any time.
Playing Lotto at two combinations a week will take you to
a sequence of 3 winning numbers twice in 56 weeks, which,
statistically speaking, is very much too-little-too-late. To stay in
the game you'd have to do better than that. At this rate you stand
a good chance of scoring 4 by the end of next year, and when
it happens—before you congratulate yourselves—please, count
your money! Buying combinations (and I hope we know that!)
doesn't multiply your chances by two, three, etc. Quite the opposite,
from there on the road leads straight into statistical hell. What we
have here is Lady Luck at work; her players are people who
put their trust in her, or rather, they trust themselves, and can do
without luck for a while. The odds that by playing just one

combination you score 5 by tomorrow stand at 1 against 7304.
The prospect of scoring 6 in a row stands at 1 against 1.533.939.
Scoring 7 exceeds the capabilities of my pocket calculator and
stands at 1 to 10 million or so, it doesn't matter. The point is that
you can count on putting your hands on the jackpot after many
hundreds of years at the game. And even then—each game begins
anew with the same odds against you. True, by raising the stakes
you can better your hand a good deal, but—I do beg your pardon.
I took to the library. Mathematics of luck is as old as our day-
dreams and presents us with an interesting reading. The ways of
predicting a score are diverse and some of them play roles in all
sorts of applications. Yet you'd better take it from me that even
the cleverest of them will not by a long shot bring you out of
the abyss of the next week's imponderable. On the other hand,

the study of math may steady your hand at raising the threshold
of your good fortunes—on the condition you know what these are.

If gambling is one of them, so be it! But to tell you the truth,
my guess is Kolmogorov was right and, on average, the prospects
don't look very good. Jackpots do happen, of course, but not
very often and almost certainly not to you. Still, life seems full
of unlikely events — one of them being that by the end of the day
you are still around. A measure of luck is needed at everything,
and if you read this you must have already exhausted a good part
of yours. But wait, no need to despair, turn a stone anywhere…
They reckon that at one time the probability the amino-acids
would coalesce into a human genome stood at 1 against 10 on
minus a number with 250 zeroes — bigger than that of all atoms
in our universe — still we exist; for a fraction of time, nonetheless.

## White Dolphins

Lovely day, a clear view from the Lion's Rock to Victoria Peak, no
haze; between one and the other a crowd of five million, all strangers.
I'm off. I keep an appointment, first such in thirty-odd years. "C.I.D.
Kowloon West; they'll know, you can't miss." Missing is easy, though.
I take my Agfa and a map, my double Ariadne's thread. You click,
then follow the clicks to the map and see where you came from.
No art, just landmarks, a side view or a shot from above like looking
down on the sea. The higher you fly, the calmer its surface. We are
to meet in Mongkok. I'm watching the sea from the top of a double-
decker bus flaunting its regular stockpile of names: Waterloo Rd.,
Prince Edward Rd., Duke Street, Essex Crescent, Dorset Gardens.
One of them is original, though — Boundary Street, a reminder of
the old demarcation line between the headland and the city which they
were to give back, though at the end they gave back on everything.
In my case that includes the Flower Market, Bird Market, Chinese
dumplings, English pastry, Skyline, Jewelry Shops, Daily Hotels.

I'm late. A red bus speeds from behind Argyle St. A tall man stands
by the exit, waving to me from afar. He steps down, his bed leg first,
white haired, dry as pepper at 95 F and 90 per cent humidity. I start
towards him. I present you the student of the 1st Senior High, Section
White Dolphins, who in '45 on May 8th ("maybe a day earlier") was
munching on a crumpled *potitza* cake while shooting rounds from his
automatic at the Castle from Rožnik above the Čad Inn. He made it
through the liberation of the city on account of his being so drunk
he was unable to move from his ditch. *Chief jing chá Kowloon Tong.*
My eyes are sore from the sweat. I smell like death. White death.
We hug awkwardly, tapping each other on our backs. Taking a good
look at me he doesn't let go: "As good as a picture!" "I smell like
plague." He gives me a glance as if I don't know what I am talking about
but then, later, as we slow down in our taxi, I start looking out for

a toilet. "Lucky you," he says, "twenty years since I could." While still
on the lookout we recite *Aurea prima* and shout: "Unsatisfactory, sit!"

This takes a while. Rush hour on Nathan Rd., we are stuck in our cab.
"Tsim Sha Tsui," he tells the cabbie, "We walk from there." In the matter
of human condition one can always depend on the Chinese I tell myself
as we push through a crowd. But not here, not now. No public places,
all shops and banks closed for lunch and bars filled up to the ceiling.
The underground Gents seems like a cellar from Grimms' *Dornröschen.*
"Give me a minute." On the platform we take a lift to the third floor.
I indulge in grateful remembrance of the city park in Sham Shui Po
and the terraced parks of Macau—a public loo in every one of them,
free of charge. We stop at a floor with a framed lithograph of a lone
woman with marvelous breasts exposed to the wind on a waterfront
pier. *Take a step in the right direction! Have a mammography now!*
"I'm not sure we came to the right place." "Wait!" He disappears and
then returns with a key. "Go—last door to your right!" Afterwards,
we sit in a waiting room; every two minutes our senses are shaken by
a discreet earthquake below. We speak softly; we take back the key.

A breath of fresh wind turns the streets bearable. We take a Star ferry
to see his old Central, up road from the Correspondents Club, now
closed. We are not sure what to do next. The only places to visit
at this time of day are the Temple and a flea market—stalls with
old photographs of Chinese prostitutes. The one in black and white
with her hair cut short, carefully studying her sex, still seems pretty,
in a belle époque way. "Did you ever ... ?" I ask. "She did not wait
for me, I'm afraid. That's her at her best, fifteen, sixteen maybe.
Then syphilis, TBC, smallpox, whatever—opium rash and a quick
ride to hell. Shame for her legs, though. Money went to the family
that sold her. Badluck, as they say." "Bad luck's no shame," I protest.
"Bad omen, I mean. Look, do you see over there?" We ride on an
uphill tram. "They are pouring concrete down their tree slopes to

prevent them from sinking. There," he points out to the mountains in the bay, "above the woodland, they're melting like sugar cubes. Bad karma for you. If you took pictures, you will carry it home." How does he know what pictures I took? "No, we just went to see dolphins. The white ones, the pinks; spent fifty dollars to see nothing ..." "No whites here for years now, except in the pictures. The pictures are old. Bad luck ..." Once a *jing chá*, always a *jing chá*. Then it strikes him I must be starving. He suggests Jockey Club. We wait for a tram, but unlike with the dolphins our waiting pays off. Soon we sip jasmine tea served on a starched table cloth, set on a revolving board with loads of *dim sum*. We eat fish and dumplings and cooked vegetables behind a big glass wall with a view of a turf course. The sprinklers wet the grass track amid the capacity crowd. Spectators, bewitched, stare at a giant screen above the south entrance showing races taking place elsewhere. Every now and then they jump up from their seats, waving their hot dogs and tickets. "Those White Dolphins of yours," I begin, "how white were they, really?" "Stone white, dusted with quick lime, at seventeen — just like the whores, but fit as a fiddle ..." He settles the bill. "Say, how do you fancy a ride to our home turf?"

We stroll under green palms and cinnamon trees; behind our backs the breeze rustles the leaves in a bamboo grove, its roots cracking the bones of a sleeping fleet of sailors. "Don't believe everything you read, most were eaten by fish. The old gang comes once a year to remember their lot — but here are the Russians!" Among the Irish crosses I notice Orthodox ones, in concrete, inscribed in Cyrillic. "Can you read?" "Natalia Bronstein," I read, "a Nurse" then, in English: *1875 †1911. Much missed by all.* — "See, she was missed, by her own here, by me back in London. You go home whenever you choose, the two of us couldn't. Here at least she's got *something*. Shame, they don't take in anymore." He wants to shake hands, but I won't let go. "Why are white dolphins a bad omen?" He licks his finger and paints a doodle in the air: "*wu gei bak gei*. White Dolphins — Bad Omen, same sign, same thing! Which devil figured that out? Can you imagine?

The Brits got them safe, then sent them all home to the pit. No way
to know until I learned Cantonese. *Badluck*."

### Remembering Hopkins

In our local Clinic stands a Tree of Health,
the branches of its richly grown crown
decorated by various inscriptions like Happiness,
Love, Good Personal Relations,
Friendship, etc. Up the tree trunk
lines of multi-colored twinkling fairy lights
lead on to them, which — in a circuit
as on big Christmas trees — then run down again
to the Tree's mighty roots, bearing labels like
Recreation, Sleep, Nutrition and Relaxation,
Giving up Bad Habits, Healthy Sexuality, Hygiene.
Lord, send the roots rain.

*Translated by Alasdair MacKinnon*

## Pred adagiem

Gledam jih na televiziji, kažejo tudi
odmore med skladbami, včasih.
Tu in tam vidimo, kako kdo zamuja,
prijazna gospodična v črnem in
rdečem ga pospremi do praznega
stola, zamudnik je v zadregi, zaveda
se svojega hrbta v domovih redkih
gledalcev, njegov hrbet se počuti
napaden, ampak na tako ljubko
spremstvo človek ne računa več niti

ob najbolj srečnih večerih. Samuel
Barber, Adagio—glasba, ki jo je smrt
državnikov napravila za pogrebni
rekvizit. Hodil sem na koncerte,
vsak teden. Albinioni, Mahler, Barber,
v tem vrstnem redu. Bila je to druga
dvorana, drug svet, brez uniformiranih
spremljevalk, brez koncertnih listov,
ki bi bili videti kot prodajni katalog—
vendar s sijajnim orkestrom. Seveda

sem zamujal, pritekel sem čez park,
odsunil težka vrata, se mimo garderobe
pognal po stopnicah in obstal pred
priprtimi vrati na balkonu. Zunaj je
bil mil pomladni večer, ki mi je dihal
s čela, ali ostra zimska noč, in nanju
so se začeli loviti zvoki nekega globljega
večera (in noči), preživetega ob jezeru,
v uti na koncu pomola, brez komarjev,
ki bi motili skladateljevo žalost. Žalost

## Before the Adagio

I watch them on television; they also show the breaks
between the musical pieces, sometimes. Now
and then I can see a latecomer arriving.
A friendly young lady in black
and red shows him
to an empty
seat.
The latecomer is embarrassed, he is aware of his back being
shown in the homes of the dwindling number
of viewers. His back feels under attack,
but such friendly accompaniment
is not something you
reckon with
even
on the happiest of evenings: Samuel Barber, Adagio –
music that the death of statesmen has made
indispensable at funerals. I used to go to
concerts every week, Albinoni,
Mahler, Barber, in that
order. That was
another
concert hall, another world, no uniformed attendants,
no concert programs looking like commercial
catalogues, but with a splendid
orchestra, nonetheless.
I was late most
of the time.
I ran
across the park, unbolted the heavy door, struggled up
the stairs past the cloak-room and stood in front
of the part-open door to the balcony.
Outside there was a mild

nekega drugega skladatelja. Naslonil
sem se na podboj, se zatopil v svoj
večer, v svojo žalost (že tretjo po vrsti),
ustrezno sestavljeno iz valov, iz šumenja
borov, iz oddaljene glasbe s plesišča.
Glasbi sta se pomešali, postali ena sama,
dišeča po borih, pluskajoča po skalah,
z enakim iztekom v tišino, v ploskanje,
v pokašljevanje. Nastopi moj trenutek.
Odrinem vrata in skoraj neviden vstopim

v dvorano. Pokima mi profesor filozofije,
ki ga ni več, malo naprej sedi moj profesor
književnosti, ki ga ni več. Zdaj, ko se ju
spominjam, tudi mene ni več. Izginem
v hipu, vendar počasi, v temo, kakor so
izginjali prizori v starih filmih. Dvorane
ni več ne glasbenikov, večeri so izumrli,
in noči. Kaj konstituira naše bivanje,
kakšna kontinuiteta, potem ko se stvari
enkrat, dvakrat, trikrat tako zelo končajo?

spring evening
breathing
on
my brow, or a sharp winter night and onto them were
beginning to get caught the sounds of some
deeper evenings (and nights)
lived through by the lake,
in the small
pavilion
by
the end of a pier with no mosquitoes to intrude on
the composer's sadness — the sadness of
some other composer. I would lean
on the door-frame, absorbed
in my own evening,
in my own
sadness
(third such in  succession), properly made up from
waves, from the rustle of the pines, from
far off music from the dance floor;
the two musics blended,
becoming a single
one, scented
with pine,
splashing on the rocks, running out the same into silence,
into applause and coughing. My moment has come,
I push open the door and almost invisible I go into
the concert hall. A nod from my professor
of Philosophy, no longer with us.
A little farther forward
sits my professor
of Literature,
no longer
with us.

Now when I see them I myself am no longer there.
I disappear in a moment, but fading out
slowly into darkness like
the scenes in old
films. No more
concert
halls,
no musicians. The evenings have died away,
the nights, too. What constitutes
our existence, what sort of
continuity, when things
end so finally — once,
twice, three
times?

# Deljena lepota

*As kingfishers catch fire…*
*G.M. Hopkins*

Vodomci v ognju … V življenju sem mogoče videl dva.
Zadnjič, ko sem že pospravljal pribor v avto, v plivkanju
klenov, v drsenju vrbovih vej čez prodnate lise valov —
tam, kjer sem stal — rdeč komet nizko nad reko, poravnan
kljun na tehtnici dneva, ki para z roko noči naslikan prizor.
Modro zlat, s škrlatom pod krili, iznenada, od nikoder!
Pade kot kamen, vstane iz krogov na vodi in že ga vzame
vijolično sivo zavetje bregov. Lepi so, res — živi od lepote,
ki se s smrtjo skoraj ne dotakne plena, vidne očem samo
kadar ubija, ko si v sekundi razdeli hip z drugačno lepoto —
srebrno zeleno, z bliskavim bokom, s hrbtom črnim kot čaj,
ki se za soncem pod žuborečo streho sveta varna med jato
prebija v večer — hvala bogu brez zavesti o tem, da je zdaj,
ta pljusk tišine pred mrakom njen zadnji.

## Divided Beauty

*As kingfishers catch fire...*
G.M. Hopkins

Kingfishers afire...I may have seen two. Once, when
I was packing my gear, with the dace hitting the surface,
the willow trees gliding on the mottled rubble-colored
waves—there, above my stand—a red comet, poised
on the scales of the day, tearing abruptly the dusk-painted
scene. Golden blue, flashing bright scarlet under the wing,
all of a sudden from nowhere! Falling like a stone, rising
in a fury of droplets—then gone, taken in by the mauve
shelter of the shore. They are beautiful. Alive with beauty,
almost not touching their prey with death—its contours
visible only when one splits the second with beauty
of another kind, a silvery green one, with its flashy sides,
its back tea-black, riding the sun under the murmuring roof
of the world, making it save into the evening in a school
of its own—Thank God, unaware that this splash of silence
before dusk is its last. ◥

# IV DELLS AND HOLLOWS

## An Improbable Incident

In the rainwater, out of
the pitch-black asphalt
of an open road the fluttering of larks
prolongs itself into the night.
Improbably now,
miracles happen
every day. Once a day
only — twice
in a lifetime.

## Bell-fright

In the mist over the winter crops
of dells and hollows
walks the absent bell ringer
to the slope of the next hill.
The ice cubes of houses
frozen to the air
as to the rim of a glass
are being warned: the evening
breaks on the ridges
and lights up in the stables
the Bethlehem stars.

## Zinnias in Bloom

Zinnias in bloom; a train
moving on, departing: maids'
work on the balcony.
An electric pole—a hedgehog
trying to climb it: a palm tree
by night. The branch of an elder-
bush dressing itself up in black:
the scent of its inflorescence
quietly glowing. Among the wild
rose petals a spider hiding from
the rain. Had it not gone into
hiding it would have stayed hidden.
Night gathers; the starlings flock
onto a sign-board: in the sky
a child from the long gone past
is happily singing. Rain descends from
the heavens; fire licks the star
by the edges. One me coming down
to lie on the earth. ✒

## Dan, ko me ljubiš

Dan, ko me ljubiš si najprej
zapomnim po sveže opranem
perilu oblakov. Poševno sonce
razpošlje zajčke čez zaboje
zelenjave; kavarne okrog trga
se odpirajo, martinčki švigajo
po stenah, ljudje se sprehajajo
z rokami v žepih. V zraku
se prevažajo tramvaji
škržata.

Knjižnice posedajo za temnimi
stekli, zamišljene v svojo
notranjost. Glasbeniki vadijo
kot da bo zdaj zdaj večer.
Ulični vogali se spominjajo
vremena in akacij v zbledeli
ljubezenski zgodbi, ki se ponovno
pripravlja med nebom
in zemljo.

Žice na nepregledni armadi
daljnovodnih stebrov, ki je zjutraj
vkorakala v mesto, se — napete
čez zemeljsko oblo — spreminjajo
v strune, ko zabrenčijo skoznje
cvetovi sinočnjih
glasov.

*Buenos Aires, 1935*

## The Day You Loved Me

I remember the day you loved me first by the newly washed
linen of clouds. A sloping sun sends its hopping
reflections over the crates of vegetables;
cafés in the town square open,
lizards are shooting up
the walls; people
walk with
hands
in their pockets; street-cars of cicadas circle the air. Libraries
brood behind the dark glass panes, absorbed in thoughts
of their interiors. Musicians practice as if evening
may come any minute. Street corners recall
the weather and the acacia trees
of a faded love story,
preparing
to break out again between the sky and the earth. Stretched
on all over the globe the wires on an inscrutable army
of power line posts marching into city since
early this morning change into strings
buzzing with blossoms
of sounds of
yesterday
night.

*Buenos Aires, 1935*

### Where Are You?

I am sitting in the doorway
under the light; the grass is darkening,
the stream below the house
sounds clearer. I've been waiting
for I don't know what, for you
to call me, for weeks. And now —
not in the house, here outside,
from over the hill, from the stream,
from the wind through the branches,
your voice sounds, soft and clear —
Where are you, what are you doing?
Moths are settling on my head.
They are drawn to what's in there
and want to get to you.

*Translated by Alasdair MacKinnon*

## Pruned, Lopped, Cut Down

Think of it,
from now on — our days
(one after another) will run on
eventfully. All of a sudden
my lighter won't spark, coffee
will run out, my Parker
won't write, what was left
in the bottle, that too,
it will run out, cheers to you!
I'm giving back none of the things
you gave me. I'm running out of them
as it is: leaves, books, feathers, planets,
pages filled with your hand, even you.
Only your despair I keep for myself.

## Stars

Stars — their comedy of errors — exaggerate. They
pull me up through my eyes, I'm moving up there,
I can hardly wait to see how it will turn out to be
when I look down on the clearing with its galactic
forest, with its shuddering glow, with its bent belt
of heavenly lake behind it — turning solid, solidifying
faster than it is diluted by distance. Into the open
one by one — with orange eyes — come stooping
creatures, alert, raising up their heads, sniffing
the air, pricking ears, drinking dew, stretching their
necks in the ecstasy of gratification. A clear sign
I am gone — they graze, the timid stars under the forest.

## Po grapah in kotanjah

Dol grede v poznojesenskem pršcu
se je zaustavil, da pretiplje žepe
za ključi in hitro vrže še en pogled
na staro hišo spodaj in potem
še enega. Nobenih avtov, nič.
Nobenih ruzakov, koles pod smreko —
kar je razločil je bila le medla
svetloba v oknih, že čez hip manj medla
v nenadnem mraku. Kaj, če obide grapo
in prek mostu skoz obletele grinte
pogleda v hišo — kaj potem? Kdorkoli
je v njej, sporoča mu, naj gre domov.
Nadihal se je mraza in odkorakal.
Slabotne in v daljavi so se v vasi
prižigale luči, a ob sestopu
se je megla pod noč tako zgostila,
da tam, kjer so se okna žage zlila
v krnico klavrne luči ni slišal
potoka izza hoj. Z "medvedovko" —
pohodno leskovko, ki zanjo stežka
bi našel dovolj majhnega medveda,
je ostrgal blato s čevljev in jo odstavil
v njen kot, ko je zagledal — razloženo
čez klaftro drv — plaščka, kapi, račko
iz plastike in ropotuljo, vsem na očeh.
Dotaknil se je mokre, mrzle račke
in brž umaknil roko. Kaj počne
tu vrtec ob tej uri? Čudno, a nič bolj
kakor ob vsaki drugi uri dneva.
Vstopil je in otrpnil. Ni mogel ven
ne noter in tako kot je obstal
tudi ni mogel več zapreti vrat.

## Of Dells and Hollows

Coming down the hill in late autumn drizzle
he stopped to search his pockets for the keys
while having one more look at his old house,
and then another; there was no car parked
under the spruce, no bikes, no hikers' gear.
All he saw was a faint light through the windows
fast getting less faint in the falling dusk.
He'd circumvent the dell and have a look
through the depleted shrubs across the bridge
and then — do what? Whoever was in there
was sending him a signal to come home.
He took a breath of cold air and marched off.
The village lights were slowly coming on,
distant and bleak. Once down there though, the fog
was spread so thick he couldn't hear the stream
from where the sawmill windows turned into
a pool of gloomy light behind the firs.
He cleaned his high boots with a walking stick —
"bear-stick" he called it — though he couldn't think
of a bear small enough to show respect
for his choice of weapon. Putting back the stick
in its old place beside the door he noticed
a plastic duck, some children's coats and hats
and a rattle toy laid on the pile of logs
for anyone's inspection. He touched the cold
wet surface of the duck and withdrew his hand.
What the heck's a nursery class doing here
at this strange hour? But then, he'd thought it strange
at any time of day. He pushed the door
and froze. He was not trying to get in
nor out; he was about to close the door
when, standing where he stood, he found he couldn't.

Namesto vrat zaprl je oči,
da se prepriča v sliko pred seboj:
v dva možaka srednjih let sedeča
v zelenih lovskih jaknah in klobukih
za hrastovo nedeljsko mizo v kotu,
ki čakata, da se prikaže z mrakom.
Lahko bi vedel. Zunaj prepoznal
je modri plašček s kapo.
                                    "Pozdravljen, oče."
Nihče ni vstal. Ni videl ju v obraz,
le slišal, in strmel v roke na mizi.
"Ker nimava življenja sva prišla,
da vidiva, kaj ti si storil s svojim."
Stekel je v noč in se ni več ustavil.

Instead, he closed his eyes to grasp the picture
of the two men in their late thirties seated
dressed in their hunters' green, with their hats on
at the long oaken table in the corner
waiting for him at dusk. And there it struck him
he half expected it — he'd recognized
the little coat and blue cap.
                              "— Hello, Dad."
No one stood up. He couldn't see their faces,
just hear them speak , their hands laid on the table.
"— Having no life of our own, we came to see
what you have done with yours." At this he turned
and ran into the night and never stopped. ◂

## Stones

One night, or late in the evening when on my way home,
I spotted in the dark — on the other side of darkness,
some distance away from the path in the dewy grass —
a shape like limbs of a bush or a small tree alive with
flashing fireflies — an apparition standing out against
the night air. I stared at the thing, which at some other
time would have turned out to be nothing but a lonely
young fern and which in spite of its palpable structure
I could not believe to be other than a mirage, a delusion
of sight to do nothing about but to retrace my steps
to the path in fear I wouldn't miss it. Later when I was

back on the road and the sky was beginning to light up
in the face of human proximity, in anticipation of what
was to come at the end of the turn where the view opened
the distance to the spot irresistibly sucked me in. Beneath
was laid the illuminated heart of the city traversed by
streams of headlights silently flowing out or diving in
and reappearing at random from under an invisible rise.
This is it! This I have seen at the top — a firefly tree
put up in the night air, at once reaching up to the stars
and stretching out below my feet — in a moment distinct
from all others, bound into an event by blurred pathways

with which nothing binds us but time — an indiscriminate
*before* and *after,* retreating in all directions like a wave-
furrow cut into the sea. *When we were still all together;*
*when we were such and such; before we* … When the cut
happens and we, not knowing it for a boundary, may
not until later, from a blade-sharp distance, make out
the patterns — our only defense against time that can no
longer be put together to make up for our lives. *This is*

*what happened, all else...* I hit the road to the valley
with the sounding cataract in the black silence behind me
bearing witness to the truth of the scene for the way...

Years after — and even that seems now a long time ago —
on the other side, by the cold coast of the Pacific, I was
hunting for stones. I like splitting them open like leaves
of a book or seeing them hit harder rock of the ground.
I searched below cedar wood going down to the shore
to the barren strata of flint stone and slate supporting roots
of sapped trunks. There on top of a volcanic plateau I saw
a small hefty boulder, inviting but hard. I weighted it up
against my chest, pushed and let drop. I recoiled perplexed
at my strength and could not believe my luck as it bounced
back and then split clean into two as if made to by a spell.

I remember, or I remembered just now, how on a stroke
of icy wind I was struck by a shooting sensation that there,
naked and in shock, in a swarm of silvery crystals, wet
from a drizzle, in the heart of that stone glimmered boughs
of a firefly tree shaped into a constellation of my home city.
I bent down to look when I saw I was bleeding, leaving behind
a speckled trail like a small soaking rodent. (Then, too, I
suddenly felt the cut from the blow.) Nothing happened,
there was nothing to see, only this: sealed annals of time
opened up to the future, and a piece of my own present,
long ready and lying in wait, was freed to pounce on me
        from out of the dark.

## On the Waterfront

I see through the waves
an oscillating monster with its own thoughts
in the deep, its invisible nerve center
thousands of miles away.

If described in a novel,
our moment would not touch the waves
until page 200.

However,
what is really delightful
this wintry morning
is their contact with the shore;
this is like sitting in the dark
in front of a garden in full bloom —

You think, like the sea and the land,
you touch me,
but you only remember
yourself.

## Birthday

To begin with, it takes her forever not to show up. Weather
is nice, birds are singing; my son waits to be picked up from
in front of a bank. The traffic gets heavy. I'm going nowhere,
I may lose them both if I move from the spot. Clouds gather.
Three o'clock, I get out of my car. Finally, tired of sticking
around, my son comes over to see what I'm up to. He takes
out his mobile; in less than ten minutes she's there. She shows
up with a flamingo in a striped cellophane; they look good, she
and the flower. She sniffs at my posy of tulips and hyacinths
through a crack in the wrapping and wants a ride home without
more delay. There, I imagine, she finds a vase for the bunch
and the flower and hides her almond cream away from her
daughter. Next, she puts on her lipstick and in her suede boots
falls fresh from the bathroom into my car as the three of us race
away past the road blocks and barriers to celebrate her birthday.

We sit in a half-empty cafe with the view of a lake. The two
sip champagne and eat up their cream cakes. After a while,
he checks at his watch and takes leave. —Duty calls, sorry,
he says and asks me to help him with his bags to a nearby hotel.
She's left waiting in the cafe. Night falls. In the dim *séparée*
lamps are switched on. I'm back, I take seat. She seems fine.
Instantly though, when we're left to ourselves, she flashes
her teeth. It's callous of one to be late, to lie that one wasn't—
it's hopeless. That's it! She's had it. She's off to the butcher's.
She cooks for her sister and her three little babies, lamb chops
with *žlikrofi*, roast beef and potatoes. She needs a recipe, fast.
Mulling it over, she changes her mind three times in a minute,
then borrows my money to buy what she needs. This reminds her
she hadn't had a square meal since morning and wants to eat out,
preferably somewhere where they serve nothing we can afford.

We take time dining. Dawn comes. It feels like a warm, mild summer day. I leave her in a group of unknowns, who, keeping off road, wait for a bus under our hay-barn. I see a tall young man she has chatted with while she was buying her lamb chops. They look at each other as if they'd never met. Then, just as I ask for her phone to speak to my son at his winter camp, I spot a dashing display taking shape in the West. Extending my hand I'm trying to make her look up, when from within a flashing wall of green clouds one after another emerge swarms of delta shaped wings flying in steady formations, like geese. Before she finds her mobile, they're gone. I throw myself on top of her as the lights, blue like some bleeping forget-me-nots, line up with the river. Toy-like bombs raise carpets of fields and trees down the bank. I cover my ears before they explode. Love, you should really
find yourself someone, I whisper. ◣

## Teeth

— Look at his teeth! She pointed out a young man
marching down the marina from the dockyards to
the yacht pier in a party of sailors. I never caught
a good look at him. I heard his laughter at which
he would throw his head backwards; I saw his black
figure in a bleached out tee-shirt with dark streaks
of sweat, and a sack over his shoulder; next, I spotted
a flashing of the metal strap on his watch which, for
the fun of it, one of them tried to pull off his wrist;
         above him circled a seagull.
She liked the teeth; throughout the evening she talked
with her mouth full and never stopped laughing like
a stream splashing over pebbles. Then the party
on the pier stopped, shaking hands, tapping shoulders,
indeterminately breaking apart in an instant. I watched
his back as he pressed on through the hooting
traffic to cross the road in a crowd of shoppers; the sack
swaying each way from his shoulder; and the seagull,
which, exasperated, pulled up and flew off with a cry,
         shooting across the rooftops.

## Trade Winds

Strange creatures — hills: summer-green, at the foot of blue
mountains, pushing their steady pace to the Alps
beneath the clear skies — water-clear
but for a pair of buzzards circling
the air over the dark of
the forest. Hushed
summer breeze
driving
out doldrums of noon. Bees happily diving into the sea
of grass, its earthy reefs, its coralline flowers.
A drop of cold sweat is winding its way
from the dark of your hairline to sit
on your brow. We eat lettuce,
fresh from the garden,
madly in love.
Tiny
mosquitos borne on the wind from the horse latitudes are
dropping, caught one by one by the shadows falling
on our bodies from a thick canopy of a walnut
tree. Trade winds are blowing, my love —
for how many nights, for how many
moon-changes, for how
many months
more.

## For the First and Last Time, Ever

I'm getting too small for my hands. My eyes tire,
my shoulders grow too narrow to carry
the breadth of the day. Whenever
I close my eyes I sense
the landscapes
in my head
sprawl
all over my body — lush, grassy, covered with
forests, intersected by rivers and railway
tracks, spangled with cities, where —
far in the east — the lights
are turning on
and the stars
roll on
towards me all at once for the first and last time,
ever. In one of the cities the two of us
stand on the bridge and hold still.
Night drips onto our hair —
Let me hold out in
my body till
morning.

## Steamers in the Rain

They congregate
like horses
tied to a stand;

rubbing their flanks
against each other, smelling
of tangerine, tobacco and seaweed;

groaning in the depths
of their fiery bellies, gurgling
draughts of silky oil.

Steaming with sweat,
already loaded with a cargo
of new scents,

sighing heavily,
slowly, as in a dream
they sink into the wind,

disappearing over the curves
of islands into their own insides
through watery curtains.

People from long ago gather
in small crowds, as with a heart-
rending song they leave

these places behind.

# ABOUT THE POET

Marjan Strojan was brought up on a small farm in Slovenia. He studied philosophy and comparative literature, and worked at one time or another as a baggage carrier and load-sheet-man at an airport, a film critic in Ljubljana, and a journalist in London. His first book of poetry *Izlet v naravo* [*An Excursion into Nature*] came out in 1989; his third book *Parniki v dežju* [*Steamers in the Rain*] received the 2000 Veronika Award for the poetry book of the year; three more volumes have followed since. Strojan has also published many translations, including *Beowulf* (1992), selections from the poetry of James Joyce (2000), Lavinia Greenlaw (2000), Robert Frost (2001), Sydney Lea, (2006), as well as Milton's *Paradise Lost* (2003, 2011) and Chaucer's *Canterbury Tales* (2012). In 1997, he published an *Antologija angleške poezije* [*Anthology of English Poetry*]. His most recent work, a translation of Shakespeare's songs from plays (*Pesmi iz iger*), to which he added his own variations on the subject (*Igre iz pesmi*), will appear in 2016.

Translations of Strojan's work have appeared in many languages. His additional honors include the Sovré Translation Prize for *Beowulf* and for Milton's *Izgubljeni raj*, and, in 2015, the distinguished France Prešeren Foundation Prize for his translation of Chaucer.